The Department of Housing and Urban Development

KNOW YOUR GOVERNMENT

The Department of Housing and Urban Development

Bob Bernotas

CHELSEA HOUSE PUBLISHERS

On the cover: Workers labor high atop the girders of a construction project. HUD is charged with overseeing the federal government's involvement in both housing and urban development, which includes the building of offices and factories as well as houses and apartments in the nation's cities.

Frontispiece: In downtown Baltimore, Maryland, the gleaming glass walls of the Charles Center rise, part of HUD-sponsored urban redevelopment.

Chelsea House Publishers
Editor-in-Chief: Remmel Nunn
Managing Editor: Karyn Gullen Browne
Copy Chief: Juliann Barbato
Picture Editor: Adrian G. Allen
Art Director: Maria Epes
Deputy Copy Chief: Mark Rifkin
Assistant Art Director: Noreen Romano
Manufacturing Manager: Gerald Levine
Systems Manager: Lindsey Ottmann
Production Manager: Joseph Romano
Production Coordinator: Marie Claire Cebrián

Know Your Government
Senior Editor: Kathy Kuhtz

Staff for THE DEPARTMENT OF HOUSING AND URBAN DEVELOPMENT
Associate Editor: Ellen Scordato
Copy Editor: Brian Sookram
Picture Researcher: Sandy Jones

Library of Congress Cataloging-in-Publication Data

Bernotas, Bob.
  The Department of Housing and Urban Development/Bob Bernotas.
    p.   cm.—(Know your government)
  Includes bibliographical references and index.
  ISBN 0-87754-841-2
       0-7910-0889-4 (pbk.)
  1. United States. Dept of Housing and Urban Development. I. Title. II. Series: Know your government (New York, N.Y.)
HT167.2.B47   1991   90-22148
353.85—dc20   CIP

CONTENTS

KNOW YOUR GOVERNMENT

The American Red Cross

The Bureau of Indian Affairs

The Central Intelligence Agency

The Commission on Civil Rights

The Department of Agriculture

The Department of the Air Force

The Department of the Army

The Department of Commerce

The Department of Defense

The Department of Education

The Department of Energy

The Department of Health and
Human Services

The Department of Housing and
Urban Development

The Department of the Interior

The Department of Justice

The Department of Labor

The Department of the Navy

The Department of State

The Department of Transportation

The Department of the Treasury

The Drug Enforcement Administration

The Environmental Protection Agency

The Equal Employment
Opportunities Commission

The Federal Aviation Administration

The Federal Bureau of Investigation

The Federal Communications Commission

The Federal Government: How it Works

The Federal Reserve System

The Federal Trade Commission

The Food and Drug Administration

The Forest Service

The House of Representatives

The Immigration and Naturalization Service

The Internal Revenue Service

The Library of Congress

The National Aeronautics and Space
Administration

The National Archives and Records
Administration

The National Foundation on the Arts
and the Humanities

The National Park Service

The National Science Foundation

The Nuclear Regulatory Commission

The Peace Corps

The Presidency

The Public Health Service

The Securities and Exchange Commission

The Senate

The Small Business Administration

The Smithsonian

The Supreme Court

The Tennessee Valley Authority

The U.S. Arms Control and
Disarmament Agency

The U.S. Coast Guard

The U.S. Constitution

The U.S. Fish and Wildlife Service

The U.S. Information Agency

The U.S. Marine Corps

The U.S. Mint

The U.S. Postal Service

The U.S. Secret Service

The Veterans Administration

CHELSEA HOUSE PUBLISHERS

INTRODUCTION

Government: Crises of Confidence

Arthur M. Schlesinger, jr.

From the start, Americans have regarded their government with a mixture of reliance and mistrust. The men who founded the republic did not doubt the indispensability of government. "If men were angels," observed the 51st Federalist Paper, "no government would be necessary." But men are not angels. Because human beings are subject to wicked as well as to noble impulses, government was deemed essential to assure freedom and order.

At the same time, the American revolutionaries knew that government could also become a source of injury and oppression. The men who gathered in Philadelphia in 1787 to write the Constitution therefore had two purposes in mind. They wanted to establish a strong central authority and to limit that central authority's capacity to abuse its power.

To prevent the abuse of power, the Founding Fathers wrote two basic principles into the new Constitution. The principle of federalism divided power between the state governments and the central authority. The principle of the separation of powers subdivided the central authority itself into three branches—the executive, the legislative, and the judiciary—so that "each may be a check on the other." The *Know Your Government* series focuses on the major executive departments and agencies in these branches of the federal government.

The Constitution did not plan the executive branch in any detail. After vesting the executive power in the president, it assumed the existence of "executive departments" without specifying what these departments should be. Congress began defining their functions in 1789 by creating the Departments of State, Treasury, and War. The secretaries in charge of these departments made up President Washington's first cabinet. Congress also provided for a legal officer, and President Washington soon invited the attorney general, as he was called, to attend cabinet meetings. As need required, Congress created more executive departments.

Setting up the cabinet was only the first step in organizing the American state. With almost no guidance from the Constitution, President Washington, seconded by Alexander Hamilton, his brilliant secretary of the treasury, equipped the infant republic with a working administrative structure. The Federalists believed in both executive energy and executive accountability and set high standards for public appointments. The Jeffersonian opposition had less faith in strong government and preferred local government to the central authority. But when Jefferson himself became president in 1801, although he set out to change the direction of policy, he found no reason to alter the framework the Federalists had erected.

By 1801 there were about 3,000 federal civilian employees in a nation of a little more than 5 million people. Growth in territory and population steadily enlarged national responsibilities. Thirty years later, when Jackson was president, there were more than 11,000 government workers in a nation of 13 million. The federal establishment was increasing at a faster rate than the population.

Jackson's presidency brought significant changes in the federal service. He believed that the executive branch contained too many officials who saw their jobs as "species of property" and as "a means of promoting individual interest." Against the idea of a permanent service based on life tenure, Jackson argued for the periodic redistribution of federal offices, contending that this was the democratic way and that official duties could be made "so plain and simple that men of intelligence may readily qualify themselves for their performance." He called this policy rotation-in-office. His opponents called it the spoils system.

In fact, partisan legend exaggerated the extent of Jackson's removals. More than 80 percent of federal officeholders retained their jobs. Jackson discharged no larger a proportion of government workers than Jefferson had done a generation earlier. But the rise in these years of mass political parties gave federal patronage new importance as a means of building the party and of rewarding activists. Jackson's successors were less restrained in the distribution of spoils. As the federal establishment grew—to nearly 40,000 by 1861—the politicization of the public service excited increasing concern.

After the Civil War the spoils system became a major political issue. High-minded men condemned it as the root of all political evil. The spoilsmen, said the British commentator James Bryce, "have distorted and depraved the mechanism of politics." Patronage, by giving jobs to unqualified, incompetent, and dishonest persons, lowered the standards of public service and nourished corrupt political machines. Office-seekers pursued presidents and cabinet secretaries without mercy. "Patronage," said Ulysses S. Grant after his presidency, "is the bane of the presidential office." "Every time I appoint someone to office," said another political leader, "I make a hundred enemies and one ingrate." George William Curtis, the president of the National Civil Service Reform League, summed up the indictment. He said,

> The theory which perverts public trusts into party spoils, making public employment dependent upon personal favor and not on proved merit, necessarily ruins the self-respect of public employees, destroys the function of party in a republic, prostitutes elections into a desperate strife for personal profit, and degrades the national character by lowering the moral tone and standard of the country.

The object of civil service reform was to promote efficiency and honesty in the public service and to bring about the ethical regeneration of public life. Over bitter opposition from politicians, the reformers in 1883 passed the Pendleton Act, establishing a bipartisan Civil Service Commission, competitive examinations, and appointment on merit. The Pendleton Act also gave the president authority to extend by executive order the number of "classified" jobs—that is, jobs subject to the merit system. The act applied initially only to about 14,000 of the more than 100,000 federal positions. But by the end of the 19th century 40 percent of federal jobs had moved into the classified category.

Civil service reform was in part a response to the growing complexity of American life. As society grew more organized and problems more technical, official duties were no longer so plain and simple that any person of intelligence could perform them. In public service, as in other areas, the all-round man was yielding ground to the expert, the amateur to the professional. The excesses of the spoils system thus provoked the counter-ideal of scientific public administration, separate from politics and, as far as possible, insulated against it.

The cult of the expert, however, had its own excesses. The idea that administration could be divorced from policy was an illusion. And in the realm of policy, the expert, however much segregated from partisan politics, can never attain perfect objectivity. He remains the prisoner of his own set of values. It is these values rather than technical expertise that determine fundamental judgments of public policy. To turn over such judgments to experts, moreover, would be to abandon democracy itself; for in a democracy final decisions must be made by the people and their elected representatives. "The business of the expert," the British political scientist Harold Laski rightly said, "is to be on tap and not on top."

Politics, however, were deeply ingrained in American folkways. This meant intermittent tension between the presidential government, elected every four years by the people, and the permanent government, which saw presidents come and go while it went on forever. Sometimes the permanent government knew better than its political masters; sometimes it opposed or sabotaged valuable new initiatives. In the end a strong president with effective cabinet secretaries could make the permanent government responsive to presidential purpose, but it was often an exasperating struggle.

The struggle within the executive branch was less important, however, than the growing impatience with bureaucracy in society as a whole. The 20th century saw a considerable expansion of the federal establishment. The Great Depression and the New Deal led the national government to take on a variety of new responsibilities. The New Deal extended the federal regulatory apparatus. By 1940, in a nation of 130 million people, the number of federal workers for the first time passed the 1 million mark. The Second World War brought federal civilian employment to 3.8 million in 1945. With peace, the federal establishment declined to around 2 million by 1950. Then growth resumed, reaching 2.8 million by the 1980s.

The New Deal years saw rising criticism of "big government" and "bureaucracy." Businessmen resented federal regulation. Conservatives worried about the impact of paternalistic government on individual self-reliance, on community responsibility, and on economic and personal freedom. The nation in effect renewed the old debate between Hamilton and Jefferson in the early republic, although with an ironic exchange of positions. For the Hamiltonian constituency, the "rich and well-born," once the advocate of affirmative government, now condemned government intervention, while the Jeffersonian constituency, the plain people, once the advocate of a weak central government and of states' rights, now favored government intervention.

In the 1980s, with the presidency of Ronald Reagan, the debate has burst out with unusual intensity. According to conservatives, government intervention abridges liberty, stifles enterprise, and is inefficient, wasteful, and arbitrary. It disturbs the harmony of the self-adjusting market and creates worse troubles than it solves. Get government off our backs, according to the popular cliché, and our problems will solve themselves. When government is necessary, let it be at the local level, close to the people. Above all, stop the inexorable growth of the federal government.

In fact, for all the talk about the "swollen" and "bloated" bureaucracy, the federal establishment has not been growing as inexorably as many Americans seem to believe. In 1949, it consisted of 2.1 million people. Thirty years later, while the country had grown by 70 million, the federal force had grown only by 750,000. Federal workers were a smaller percentage of the population in 1985 than they were in 1955—or in 1940. The federal establishment, in short, has not kept pace with population growth. Moreover, national defense and the postal service account for 60 percent of federal employment.

Why then the widespread idea about the remorseless growth of government? It is partly because in the 1960s the national government assumed new and intrusive functions: affirmative action in civil rights, environmental protection, safety and health in the workplace, community organization, legal aid to the poor. Although this enlargement of the federal regulatory role was accompanied by marked growth in the size of government on all levels, the expansion has taken place primarily in state and local government. Whereas the federal force increased by only 27 percent in the 30 years after 1950, the state and local government force increased by an astonishing 212 percent.

Despite the statistics, the conviction flourishes in some minds that the national government is a steadily growing behemoth swallowing up the liberties of the people. The foes of Washington prefer local government, feeling it is closer to the people and therefore allegedly more responsive to popular needs. Obviously there is a great deal to be said for settling local questions locally. But local government is characteristically the government of the locally powerful. Historically, the way the locally powerless have won their human and constitutional rights has often been through appeal to the national government. The national government has vindicated racial justice against local bigotry, defended the Bill of Rights against local vigilantism, and protected natural resources against local greed. It has civilized industry and secured the rights of labor organizations. Had the states' rights creed prevailed, there would perhaps still be slavery in the United States.

The national authority, far from diminishing the individual, has given most Americans more personal dignity and liberty than ever before. The individual freedoms destroyed by the increase in national authority have been in the main the freedom to deny black Americans their rights as citizens; the freedom to put small children to work in mills and immigrants in sweatshops; the freedom to pay starvation wages, require barbarous working hours, and permit squalid working conditions; the freedom to deceive in the sale of goods and securities; the freedom to pollute the environment—all freedoms that, one supposes, a civilized nation can readily do without.

"Statements are made," said President John F. Kennedy in 1963, "labelling the Federal Government an outsider, an intruder, an adversary. . . . The United States Government is not a stranger or not an enemy. It is the people of fifty states joining in a national effort. . . . Only a great national effort by a great people working together can explore the mysteries of space, harvest the products at the bottom of the ocean, and mobilize the human, natural, and material resources of our lands."

So an old debate continues. However, Americans are of two minds. When pollsters ask large, spacious questions—Do you think government has become too involved in your lives? Do you think government should stop regulating business?—a sizable majority opposes big government. But when asked specific questions about the practical work of government—Do you favor social security? unemployment compensation? Medicare? health and safety standards in factories? environmental protection? government guarantee of jobs for everyone seeking employment? price and wage controls when inflation threatens?—a sizable majority approves of intervention.

In general, Americans do not want less government. What they want is more efficient government. They want government to do a better job. For a time in the 1970s, with Vietnam and Watergate, Americans lost confidence in the national government. In 1964, more than three-quarters of those polled had thought the national government could be trusted to do right most of the time. By 1980 only one-quarter was prepared to offer such trust. But by 1984 trust in the federal government to manage national affairs had climbed back to 45 percent.

Bureaucracy is a term of abuse. But it is impossible to run any large organization, whether public or private, without a bureaucracy's division of labor and hierarchy of authority. And we live in a world of large organizations. Without bureaucracy modern society would collapse. The problem is not to abolish bureaucracy, but to make it flexible, efficient, and capable of innovation.

Two hundred years after the drafting of the Constitution, Americans still regard government with a mixture of reliance and mistrust—a good combination. Mistrust is the best way to keep government reliable. Informed criticism is the means of correcting governmental inefficiency, incompetence, and arbitrariness; that is, of best enabling government to play its essential role. For without government, we cannot attain the goals of the Founding Fathers. Without an understanding of government, we cannot have the informed criticism that makes government do the job right. It is the duty of every American citizen to know our government—which is what this series is all about.

A HUD program that helps pay the interest on mortgages aided the construction of the Windsor Apartments in Wilmington, Delaware. The apartment
complex is one of many built with the help of one of HUD's programs for low-
cost housing.

ONE

"To Rebuild the Entire Urban United States"

T he forces of urbanization and industrialization have had a profound effect on 20th-century American society. Both phenomena have been closely interconnected and each has contributed to the growth of the other. In many ways, the expansion of industry in the United States spawned the rise of the modern American city.

In the late 19th century, the development of steam- and electric-powered engines and the introduction of efficient mass production techniques fueled the growth of new industries, which began to attract great masses of workers to the cities of the Northeast and Midwest. These rapidly growing enterprises, such as steel production, oil refining, large-scale manufacturing of all types (especially automotive), and food processing, to name a few, required large numbers of people working together in one place. Urban centers filled with migrants from rural areas who saw that they could earn more money working in the factories than they could "down on the farm." The cities also became magnets for waves of immigrants from European countries, who were convinced that industrial America held out the dual promise of prosperity and freedom. As a consequence, these booming urban centers bulged with great and growing concentrations of industrial workers living close to one another— an unprecedented development in the United States.

New cities sprang up as modern industries emerged. Workers in factories that turned out large, complicated products such as refrigerators and tractors assembled them from many small parts, which were manufactured in other factories. For example, the automotive industry created the tire industry; in a sense, Detroit gave birth to Akron, Ohio. Out of the manufacturing sector of the economy grew the shipping industry, for the goods produced in the factories had to be distributed throughout the nation, and ultimately the world. As a result, many cities became major railroad centers or seaports, creating more jobs, and crowding even more new workers into the nation's expanding urban centers.

As the 20th century progressed, the United States was well on its way to becoming a nation of cities. In 1900, only about 40 percent of Americans lived in urban areas; by 1960, that figure had jumped to 70 percent. Observing this trend, some population experts predicted that 80 percent of the nation's population increase between the years 1965 and 2000 will have occurred in urban areas.

In the 1970s and 1980s, the decline of the steel and automotive industries, the economic cornerstones of the Northeast and Midwest, was reflected in the slowed, and in some cases diminishing, growth rate in the cities of these former industrial heartlands. However, the overall process of urbanization in America has not stopped. New high-tech industries, which include electronics, communications, and computers, have created booming urban centers in the so-called Sun Belt of the South and Southwest, and on the Pacific Coast.

But industrial expansion and urban growth brought with them new social problems and volatile political issues. Slums, pollution, unemployment, and the general demand for a wide range of social services precipitated a gradual expansion of the federal bureaucracy throughout the 20th century. The federal government, however slowly, began to realize that in a nation of cities, urban problems are truly national problems.

The expansion of the federal bureaucracy reveals the changing attitude of the national government and the American people. In the early 1900s, most political leaders held fast to the notion of *laissez-faire*, the idea that government should not intervene in running the economy. Nevertheless, in 1903 Congress established the Department of Commerce and Labor. Ten years later, it had become clear that the interests of employers and workers were not identical but instead often in opposition. And so, in 1913 the single department was split, creating two separate departments, Commerce and Labor.

Over the years, the establishment of new cabinet departments, such as Health, Education, and Welfare in 1953—which in 1979 was renamed the

16

An aerial view of Boston's West End before urban renewal reveals rows of decaying tenements and aging factories. Part of HUD's mission from the outset has been the revitalization of areas stricken with urban blight.

Department of Health and Human Services—Transportation in 1966, Energy in 1977, and Education in 1979, has reflected the federal government's growing concern for the social impact of economic growth, and in particular, its impact on cities. In his March 1965 Message on the Cities, President Lyndon B. Johnson called attention to these problems of growth and warned that government must meet the issue head-on, without delay: "In the remainder of this century—in less than 40 years—urban population will double, city land use will double. . . . It is as if we had 40 years to rebuild the entire urban United States." By the end of August 1965, after 11 years of political debate and struggle, Congress enacted legislation to establish the Department of Housing and Urban Development (HUD), the principal federal agency responsible for programs concerned with housing needs, fair housing opportunities, and development of the nation's communities.

HUD's Mission

HUD was created to carry out a wide range of tasks—administrative, political, economic, and social. Administratively, HUD brought together under one roof the various federal programs that assist housing and community development—programs such as low-rent public housing, mortgage insurance, urban renewal, and other forms of assistance to localities. Many policymakers believed that these existing programs could be more effective if they were organized by one authority. After all, the problems of urban America are not fragmented and distinct, but complex and interconnected, requiring a coordinated policy response. Further, a single administrative department would serve as a focal point for policy research and innovation and would provide strong, unified leadership in carrying out new national programs for urban development.

Politically, the creation of HUD gave representation in the president's cabinet to the 130 million Americans who, at that time, were city dwellers. From the beginning of the debate about a national urban policy, proponents of a new federal department argued that urban residents deserved the same kind of cabinet-level voice already enjoyed by farmers in the Department of Agriculture, businesspeople in the Department of Commerce, and trade union members in the Department of Labor. In part, HUD was conceived as a means of correcting a perceived imbalance of power at the highest level of the federal government and of constituting urban residents into a loose interest group.

An additional dimension to HUD's political mission arises because the great majority of black Americans live in urban areas. HUD's advocates argued that the creation of this department would help to demonstrate the federal government's commitment to the concerns of black Americans. It is, therefore, noteworthy that HUD came into being during the peak of the civil rights movement and in the wake of the first wave of ghetto uprisings. The first secretary of HUD, Robert C. Weaver, was the first black to serve in a president's cabinet.

Economically, HUD supports the housing construction industry and the lending institutions that help make home building profitable. Its various programs of financial grants, subsidies, mortgage insurance, and direct loans help to finance many types of home building, as well as more wide-ranging programs for urban development. HUD-backed projects also provide many benefits to the local and national economy. Land that is put to profitable use can produce taxable revenue, which broadens a community's tax base. When a city takes in more taxes, it can spend more on education, police and fire protection, and other social programs that make life in the city better for its residents. A

Robert C. Weaver, the first secretary of HUD, speaks to the press in front of a cooperative rehabilitation venture between HUD and New York City. HUD has always striven to work closely with municipal housing departments to create low-cost housing.

healthy, active construction industry creates jobs and supports workers in associated trades, such as plumbing, electrical installation, and landscaping.

Finally, there is HUD's social mission. Simply put, HUD's goal is to provide a decent, affordable place to live for every American, regardless of income level or any other condition. In addition, HUD is charged with protecting the right of all Americans to live where they choose, without being subjected to racial discrimination or any other kind of illegal restriction.

What Does HUD Do?

HUD carries out its multifaceted mission through the many programs it administers. These programs can be grouped into six general categories:

1. HUD insures mortgages for single- and multifamily dwellings and loans for home improvement and the purchase of manufactured, or mobile, homes.

2. HUD channels funds from investors into the mortgage industry through the Government National Mortgage Association.

3. HUD makes direct loans for the construction or rehabilitation of housing projects for the elderly or handicapped.

4. HUD provides housing subsidies for low- and moderate-income families.

5. HUD provides grants to states and communities for community development activities.

6. HUD promotes equal housing opportunities by enforcing federal civil rights and fair-housing laws.

In its first year in operation, fiscal year 1966, HUD's budget stood at just under $4.5 billion, placing it seventh in funding among the 11 cabinet departments then existing. Its budget was more than that of the departments of Labor, the Interior, Justice, and State. At that time the Department of Defense received the most funding of all cabinet departments, with a budget of nearly $49.5 billion. Through the years HUD has maintained that same relative position in the cabinet. Its budget for fiscal 1989, for example, was approximately $15 billion, placing it ninth among the then 14 departments.

A senior citizen proudly surveys her new apartment in the Vistula Manor, which opened on December 1, 1967, in Toledo, Ohio. The Toledo Metropolitan Housing Authority used HUD funds to study design features and build Vistula Manor—the nation's first public housing specifically suited to senior citizens and physically challenged tenants.

Virtually all of HUD's budgetary dollars are spent on programs within three areas. Housing programs take up the largest share, 57 percent. Of the remainder, 22 percent of the budget supports programs concerned with community planning and development, 17 percent is devoted to public and Indian housing programs, and the remaining 4 percent is divided among all of the department's other programs.

From its inception HUD has had a relatively small staff. Its original work force numbered fewer than 13,600 employees, making it the second smallest cabinet department. Many of its major programs, especially in the areas of public housing and community development, are designed to be administered by the recipients of HUD funds, such as state and local agencies, rather than by the HUD staff. HUD oversees these types of programs instead of directly administering them.

In fiscal year 1988 (from October 1, 1987 to September 30, 1988), HUD employees worked a total of 13,214 *staff-years*. (A staff-year is equivalent to the working time and paid leave of one employee for one year; a department's staff-year figure is generally the same as the size of its full-time work force for the given year.) In 1988, HUD employees totaled 3,131 staff-years in the department's Washington, D.C., headquarters and 10,083 in the 10 regional offices and 71 field offices throughout the United States. HUD's staffing level reached its peak in fiscal 1980 at 17,401 staff-years, decreasing steadily through 1986 to 11,998, and increasing slightly in 1987 and 1988.

When the number of HUD staffers declined during the mid-1980s, much of the work that formerly was done in-house by department personnel was either contracted out or delegated to other agencies. HUD's staff performs only about two-thirds of the department's work. For example, banks and other lending institutions process most of the applications for Federal Housing Administration loans at no cost to HUD. In the end, lending institutions or building contractors do nearly half—43 percent—of all home mortgage insurance work.

Under the level of funding, just more than $23 billion, provided during fiscal year 1991, approximately 10 million households received direct benefits through HUD's mortgage insurance and housing subsidy programs. Millions more benefit from programs such as community development grants. In addition, HUD policies affect the national economy through their influence on the mortgage and home-building industries. Because its programs are so extensive and housing is extremely important to both individuals and the nation, gauging the full impact of HUD's programs on the American people is difficult. The department's actions touch, either directly or indirectly, virtually every person in the United States.

21

Jacob Riis took this 1888 photograph of Bandits' Roost, a squalid haunt of tenement dwellers in New York City. Riis's pioneering photojournalism made Americans aware of the shocking state of the urban poor and contributed to the federal government's first expression of interest in urban problems—a study grant of $20,000.

TWO

The Birth of HUD

In 1892, the federal government expressed concern for the problems of urban life for the first time in the nation's history when Congress provided $20,000 for a special investigation of *urban blight* (urban blight refers to the economic and physical decay and deterioration of areas within a city) in four large American cities. Although cities had grown tremendously throughout the 19th century, many Americans remained unaware of what life was like in these expanding metropolises. That state of affairs changed in 1891, when photographer-journalist Jacob Riis published his graphic account of life in the slums of New York City, *How the Other Half Lives*. The book brought readers face-to-face with starving families living three to four in a room amid squalid conditions and awakened the American public to the problems of the cities. In part, the outcry the book raised prompted the congressional investigation. However, the report did not produce any meaningful efforts to deal with the disturbing conditions that Riis had documented.

The first program of federal housing assistance was instituted during World War I when Congress appropriated funds to provide housing for workers in major shipyards and munitions plants. After the war, these buildings were sold to private owners. Until the 1930s, the federal government played almost no role in the society's efforts to house its people.

The Foundations of HUD: 1933–49

The stock market crash of October 1929 precipitated a decade of economic devastation, known as the Great Depression. Stock market investors found themselves penniless or in debt as the value of their holdings evaporated when stock prices plunged. Businesses could not raise money by selling stocks to maintain their growth. Banks that had invested their money unprofitably or loaned money that was not repaid closed their doors, leaving depositors with nothing. As less money was available, prices plunged, causing an economic phenomenon called deflation. Once-profitable businesses barely could keep themselves in the black. Millions of workers in every sector of American industry lost their jobs.

The entire structure of the housing market in the United States crumbled. There was an acute shortage of money available to finance new construction. Thousands of builders realized that no one could get a mortgage to pay for a new house and virtually overnight they stopped work, leaving millions of construction workers jobless. Many of the unemployed could not keep up the mortgage payments on their own homes and had to be evicted. When an individual borrows money to buy property, such as a car or a house, the property becomes the *collateral* for the loan. If the borrower *defaults* (fails to pay the money back), the lender can take possession of the property in a process called *foreclosure*—a terrifying word to countless families during the Great Depression. By 1933, more than 1.5 million homes had been foreclosed, and once-proud homeowning families were forced to move into slums, or worse, became homeless, living in cars, trailers, tents, shacks, and shanty-towns.

For more than three years the administration of President Herbert Hoover did little to ameliorate the devastation wrought by the depression. By the time President Franklin Delano Roosevelt took office in March 1933, housing and construction were at their lowest points. *Housing starts* (the number of new houses under construction), which had reached a peak in 1925 at 937,000 units, fell to 330,000 in 1930; by 1933, they had plummeted to 93,000. Foreclosures were wiping out homeowners at the rate of 1,000 a day. Banks had thousands of unsalable houses on their hands and no money in their vaults.

Immediately upon his inauguration, Roosevelt began to push through Congress a package of legislation designed to prop up the nation's beleaguered economic institutions—his New Deal. This legislation created several agencies and administrations to accomplish its purpose, including the Public Works Administration (PWA), which financed a wide range of public construction

A homeless family drags its belongings down the road in Oklahoma in 1939. During the Great Depression, President Franklin D. Roosevelt's administration formed the Home Owners' Loan Corporation (HOLC) to help families pay their mortgages and prevent homelessness. The HOLC was later incorporated into the Federal Housing Administration (FHA), a precursor of HUD.

projects—bridges, highways, airports, hospitals, and sewage plants, as well as low-cost housing and slum clearance.

As an emergency measure, Congress and Roosevelt created the Home Owners' Loan Corporation (HOLC) to stem the tide of foreclosures, which had totaled 26,000 in the month of June 1933. Between 1933 and 1936, the HOLC paid off the short-term, high-interest mortgages of more than a million distressed homeowners and refinanced these mortgages with long-term loans at 3 percent interest. By getting money into the banks, the HOLC put the insolvent home finance industry back on its feet. Of even greater importance, it was a lifesaver for millions of Americans who were facing foreclosure and eviction from their homes.

In 1933, President Roosevelt expressed interest in forming a government agency that could stimulate building by relying on private enterprise rather than government spending. His idea was realized in the first great landmark in New Deal housing legislation, the 1934 National Housing Act, which created the Federal Housing Administration (FHA). Under the FHA mortgage insurance program, a lending institution is guaranteed that the mortgage it makes for the purchase, construction, or repair of a home will be repaid even if the borrower defaults. In this way, the FHA removed the risk to banks from home mortgage loans.

Previously, the typical mortgage required a high down payment, a short term to pay back the loan, and what are known as *balloon payments*, disproportionately large, and often financially prohibitive, payments that come due at the end of the loan's term. The FHA program encouraged lenders to make mortgages on terms more favorable to the borrower, notably, by requiring smaller down payments, allowing longer repayment periods, and scheduling gradual, equal payments. FHA mortgage insurance, therefore, helped restructure the way people borrowed and repaid money for home purchases. Unlike the HOLC, the FHA was enacted as a permanent agency, and so represented the first real commitment on the part of the federal government to a long-term housing policy. Nearly six decades since its creation, the FHA continues to put homeownership within the reach of a greatly broadened segment of the population.

FHA mortgage insurance did not address the needs of those too poor to purchase a home; it never was intended to do so. Roosevelt envisioned the program less as a way to aid slum dwellers than as a means of reviving the sick housing industry—nearly a third of the unemployed had worked in the building trades. Slum clearance and government-subsidized housing were relatively low priorities on the New Deal agenda. As late as 1937, the PWA's Housing Division had started only 49 projects with a total of fewer than 25,000 residential units. Critics of the PWA's disappointing performance began calling for the creation of a separate federal agency that would undertake the creation of low-cost housing as a permanent government activity.

The 1937 United States Housing Act was created, in its own words, to make housing available to "families who are in the lowest income groups and who cannot afford to pay enough to cause private enterprise . . . to build an adequate supply of decent, safe, and sanitary dwellings for their use." To accomplish this, the law provided for the establishment of local public housing

The 1937 United States Housing Act authorized the creation of local public housing authorities to build low-income housing. Two years later, the New York City Housing Authority opened this 3,100-unit project in Queensbridge, New York, built under the provisions of the U.S. Housing Act.

authorities. These agencies were authorized to sell bonds backed by the federal government as a means of financing the development of housing for low-income families. Local communities, through these housing authorities, would build, own, and manage these low-rent housing projects. The federal government, through the Public Housing Administration (PHA), would subsidize the cost of development and construction. The coming of World War II brought the public housing program to a temporary halt, however, because construction materials were diverted to the even more urgent needs of the war effort.

The federal government's housing policy was growing, although in an uncoordinated, piecemeal manner. In 1942, President Roosevelt, drawing on his war powers, issued an executive order creating the National Housing Agency. The new agency, which collected the FHA, the PHA, and 14 other housing-related agencies under a single administrative roof, was intended as a temporary measure, a wartime attempt to streamline the burgeoning, and costly, federal bureaucracy.

During World War II, almost all federal housing programs ground to a halt, except those devoted to housing for the war effort, such as this project in Tampa, Florida, for army enlisted personnel and their dependents.

During the war, masses of workers seeking jobs in the defense industry had migrated to the cities. After the war, they were joined by the huge number of returning veterans, which created a severe housing shortage. As policymakers turned their attention toward this growing problem, they began to see the advantages of coordinating all federal nonfarm housing programs within a single agency. So, in 1947 the National Housing Agency was made into a permanent fixture and renamed the Housing and Home Finance Agency (HHFA). The HHFA was the direct precursor of HUD.

Through the 1930s, the economic deprivation wrought by the depression devastated the nation's cities. In the early 1940s, wartime needs had to take priority over urban maintenance and improvement. By the late 1940s, urban America had severely deteriorated. This evident decay, combined with the postwar housing shortage, prompted the passage of the most ambitious housing legislation ever enacted, the Housing Act of 1949.

Vowing to help realize "the goal of a decent home and a suitable living environment for every American family," the law authorized the construction of 810,000 new public housing units in the next 6 years. Through the 1950s, however, this renewed and expanded federal commitment to public housing was frustrated by Congresses that refused to vote funding for housing, the opposition of local authorities, and the resistance of the Eisenhower administration. As late as 1973, when President Nixon imposed a moratorium on public housing projects, the 1949 target figure of 810,000 units still had not been achieved.

The Creation of HUD: 1954–65

The 1950s were marked by a reduction in the federal commitment to programs concerned with housing and the needs of cities. President Eisenhower was opposed to the growth of the federal government and its interference in what he deemed essentially municipal and state problems. He was notably unenthusiastic about public housing and slum clearance, and although he did not try to abolish these programs, he consistently recommended low levels of funding for them. The one significant achievement in housing policy during the Eisenhower years was the incorporation of senior citizens into the public housing program. For example, in 1956, Congress provided for the admission of single aged persons into public housing, gave additional funding to local authorities for the benefit of senior citizen tenants, and authorized higher construction costs for their specially designed houses.

Ironically, it was during this era of federal disinterest in urban problems that the notion of a cabinet-level department of urban affairs began to gain steam. The idea was not new. In 1912, Philip Kates, an attorney in Tulsa, Oklahoma, wrote an article for the journal *American City* in which he suggested the establishment of a federal Department of Municipalities. "Municipal government," he wrote, "has been our national failure." Kates conceived of the department primarily as a study group that would collect information on urban conditions throughout the world and make recommendations to local authorities. President Woodrow Wilson expressed interest in the idea, but nothing came of it.

Through the next four decades, the idea of a federal agency concerned with the interests and problems of cities remained alive, although dormant. In 1935, the National Resources Board, a New Deal policy-planning agency, inaugurated a study of "the role of the urban community in the national economy" at the urging of one of its members, the political scientist Charles E. Merriam. Merriam's study committee concluded that a Department of Urban Affairs was needed to "appraise and evaluate the conditions and progress of urban life and the success or failure of policies designed to deal with urban problems." However, its parent body, the National Resources Board, felt this proposal was too controversial. Indeed, when the committee's final report was published in 1937, President Roosevelt stated that "it is not the business of the United States Government to assume responsibility for the solution of purely local problems." Even within the liberal Roosevelt administration, the prevailing view was that the problems of America's cities should not be the focus of federal attention.

The first legislative attempt to create a cabinet department dealing with urban issues occurred in 1954 when Representative J. Arthur Younger of California introduced a bill in Congress proposing the establishment of a Department of Urbiculture. By coining this odd term, *urbiculture*, Younger intended to draw a parallel with the Department of Agriculture. As far back as the Wilson administration, urban advocates had called for, in the words of Harold S. Buttenheim, publisher of *American City*, a federal bureau to "perform for cities services somewhat analogous to those performed for rural sections by the Department of Agriculture."

The nation's rural sector had enjoyed cabinet representation since 1889. In the age of urbanization, Younger and his supporters insisted, the cities were entitled to equal status. It was a compelling argument that helped to convince many people in and out of government. Certainly the Department of Agriculture had increased the productivity of rural America and raised the standard of living of both the American farmer and the nation as a whole. A Department of Urbiculture, many hoped, could do the same for the cities and the nation.

Cabinet status brings with it certain built-in benefits. A cabinet secretary has a significant measure of prestige and authority, which means increased clout when dealing with Congress, other departments, the public, and the press. Cabinet status also promises, at least in theory, greater access to the president. As William L. C. Wheaton, a professor of city planning and an early advocate of cabinet status for urban affairs, argued, such a department would "secure a seat at the bargaining table in the White House where the Federal pie is cut up and divided. In Washington, unfortunately, the flaming sword of truth is a poor substitute for the broad axe of influence." In practice, however, a cabinet secretary's influence can vary greatly with the executive style of a president, the pressure of events that may occupy the president's attention, and the confidence that a president has in a particular secretary.

Bills similar to Younger's 1954 proposal were introduced in each succeeding Congress but nothing came of them. By 1959, some sort of action seemed likely. The House Committee on Government Operations reported favorably on a bill introduced by Representative Dante Fascell of Florida that would create a Commission on Metropolitan Problems and Urban Development to investigate urban dilemmas and recommend federal policies. The full House did not act on the bill, although the Senate passed a similar measure. Senator Joseph Clark of Pennsylvania was exasperated by the House's inaction. "A visitor from outer space," he mused, "looking at the structure of our Federal Government, would surely conclude that America is still a rural nation, with rural problems the dominant concern."

The situation changed greatly with the inauguration of President John F. Kennedy. Kennedy became the first president to endorse the idea that the interests and problems of the nation's cities should be represented at the cabinet table. In his first State of the Union address in January 1961 he declared, "Our national household is cluttered with unfinished and neglected tasks. Our cities are engulfed in squalor. . . . We still have 25 million Americans living in substandard homes. A new housing program under a new Housing and Urban Affairs Department will be needed this year."

In April, Representative Fascell and Senator Clark introduced identical bills, based on the president's recommendation, in their respective houses of Congress. These measures proposed that the existing Housing and Home Finance Agency and its constituent parts (the Public Housing Administration, the Urban Renewal Administration, the Federal Housing Administration, the Federal National Mortgage Association, and the Community Facilities Admin-

31

President Kennedy signs the 1961 Housing Act into law. Behind him stand (left to right, first row) Robert C. Weaver, Housing and Home Finance administrator; Marie McGuire, commissioner of Public Housing; and Vice-president Lyndon Johnson. Although he supported federal housing programs, Kennedy found that his efforts to found a cabinet-level department of housing were not successful.

istration) be unified and expanded into a cabinet-level Department of Urban Affairs and Housing.

Opponents of the measure argued that the creation of this federal department would undermine local and state initiatives. They still refused to accept the idea that the problems of cities affected and produced problems for the nation as a whole. In early 1962, the House Rules Committee refused to grant a rule for floor action on Fascell's bill, thus killing it. The administration then tried a new tactic. Under the Reorganization Act of 1949, the president may submit to Congress plans to reorganize the executive branch by transferring, abolishing, or consolidating agency functions. So, six days after the Rules Committee action, Kennedy submitted his Reorganization Plan No. 1 of 1962, which would have created a cabinet-level Department of Urban Affairs and Housing. In February, by a vote of 264 to 150, the House rejected the administration's proposal.

After President Kennedy's assassination in November 1963, his successor, President Lyndon Johnson, continued the fight for a new cabinet department. In his Housing Message of January 1964, Johnson argued that "if we are to deal successfully with the complex problems of our urban and suburban communities, we need governmental machinery designed for the 1960s, not the 1940s. . . . Action to convert the Housing and Home Finance Agency into an executive department is long overdue." Bills were introduced calling for the establishment of such a department, but, as before, they failed to pass Congress.

A number of factors had combined to stymie what should have been a natural and urgently needed action—the upgrading of urban affairs to cabinet-level importance. First, congressional opponents consistently raised the specter of that time-honored political bogeyman—bureaucracy. For example, in 1962, when the Rules Committee blocked the bill that the Kennedy administration had backed, it gave as its reason "bad bureaucratic organization." Critics continually insisted that the new department would be an unnecessary, costly, and inefficient expansion of that old villain, "big government."

In response, supporters argued that only a cabinet secretary would have sufficient authority to deal effectively with the many and multifaceted problems confronting the cities. They pointed out that existing programs (such as mortgage insurance, public housing, and urban renewal) would be better organized, and so more effective, if they were brought together under a unified executive authority, which could add new programs if and when they became necessary.

There also were some unspoken biases against the proposed department. American culture, despite large-scale urbanization, continued to maintain a nostalgic attachment to images of rural and small-town life. More concretely, as late as the 1950s and 1960s, representatives from rural areas wielded a disproportionately large share of influence in Congress, especially as powerful committee chairs. Thus, advocates of cabinet status for urban affairs had to overcome persistent antiurban cultural and political biases.

(*continued on page 36*)

Robert C. Weaver: HUD's First Secretary

Robert C. Weaver took office as the first secretary of the Department of Housing and Urban Development on January 18, 1966. For 30 years he had been involved, at both the state and federal levels, with housing and urban policy. For the previous five years, Weaver had served as head of the Housing and Home Finance Agency (HHFA). He was the author of numerous widely respected books and articles on housing and urban affairs and was well known for his studies of the effects of racial discrimination on urban life.

As the top housing official in Washington, it was natural that Weaver be elevated to secretary of the new department; however, he was also the highest-ranking *black* person in the federal government. During the legislative battle to create HUD, President Kennedy disclosed that he had every intention of appointing Weaver to the new post, which would make him the first black cabinet member in U.S. history. Kennedy's bold announcement, however, eroded support for the proposed department among conservative southern Democrats in Congress. When the Johnson administration finally succeeded in creating HUD in 1965, Weaver was still head of HHFA and so still first in line for the job of secretary. His credentials and experience nearly ensured his confirmation by the Senate.

Once the creation of HUD was achieved, however, Johnson acted strangely—and some people thought cruelly—toward the man who deserved to pilot the brand-new department. For months, Johnson delayed naming Weaver as secretary of HUD and engaged in a charade of considering hundreds of other possible appointees. Political observers were confounded; the sooner that Weaver was appointed, they argued, the sooner he could get on with the difficult task of consolidating formerly independent sections of the executive branch into a unified cabinet department. Perhaps by delaying the appointment and examining such a long list of names, Johnson intended to strengthen Weaver's position as the outstanding candidate for the job. Still, no one who knew Robert Weaver's record needed to be convinced that he was the best person to be HUD secretary. Finally, Johnson named Weaver as his appointee, and many observers breathed a sigh of relief.

During his three years as HUD's first secretary (1966–68), Weaver accomplished a great deal. The Model Cities program, several new measures to house low- and moderate-income families, and a major research program were added to the government's urban policy arsenal. The aim of the controversial urban renewal program was shifted from razing slums to rehabilitating

Before taking the helm at HUD, Robert C. Weaver held many high-ranking positions in New York State housing agencies. After his resignation from government, he became president of Baruch College for two years, then embarked on a career as a professor at the City University of New York. He was eventually named the distinguished professor of urban affairs at Hunter College.

that many of its programs were designed to redress the grievances of black Americans. All in all, Weaver built the nascent HUD into a unified, coherent department.

Weaver's leadership and vision proved a difficult act for subsequent HUD secretaries to follow. Nixon's first appointee, George Romney (1968–73), inherited a package of ambitious programs developed during Weaver's tenure and administered them with vigor and commitment. However, his successor, James Lynn (1973–75), presided over Nixon's wholesale dismantling of federal housing programs. During the Ford presidency, HUD suffered from the legacy of Nixon's housing moratorium; Secretary Carla Hills (1975–77) struggled vainly to pull the department out of its state of confusion and low morale. The economic recession of the Carter years hampered the attempts of secretaries Patricia Harris (1977–79) and Moon Landrieu (1979–81) to revive and expand HUD's activities in any significant way. During Samuel Pierce's long tenure (1981–89), HUD's programs were gutted by Reagan's budget cutters. Revelations of conflict of interest, mismanagement, and fraud under Pierce's stewardship left his successor, Bush appointee Jack Kemp (1989–), with the difficult tasks of reforming HUD's operations and rebuilding its image with Congress and the public.

them. Public housing was improved and, in 1968, greatly expanded. The independent-minded Federal Housing Administration (FHA) was incorporated as a loyal and energetic component of the new department. Finally, with Weaver at the helm, HUD made the government more responsive to the civil rights movement, because Weaver made sure

(*continued from page 33*)

There also was an element of racism at work. By the mid-1950s, an increasingly large portion of the public housing population consisted of black families on public assistance. Public housing and urban programs in general were perceived by many legislators, particularly conservative southern Democrats, as "black programs," and they adamantly opposed giving cabinet-level status to the interests of blacks.

Moreover, in 1962, President Kennedy announced that he intended to appoint a black man, HHFA head Robert C. Weaver, as secretary of the new department. Kennedy hoped that his announcement might dampen congressional resistance, because opponents would clearly appear to be voting on purely racial lines. The idea backfired—all but two southern Democratic senators and four southern Democratic representatives voted against the

Department of Urban Renewal officials in Chicago, Illinois, contemplate plans submitted by prospective redevelopers of a South Side slum in October 1964. One year later, HUD was formed and took over the coordination of federal housing and urban redevelopment programs.

36

President Lyndon Johnson (right) and Vice-president Hubert H. Humphrey were in office to witness the formation of HUD, which was due largely to Johnson's legislative efforts.

proposed department. "I played it too cute," Kennedy admitted. "It was so obvious it made them mad."

But President Johnson remained undaunted, even in the face of these annual setbacks. In his 1965 State of the Union address, Johnson called attention to the needs of urban America and asserted, "A Department of Housing and Urban Development will be needed to spearhead this effort in our cities." He further elaborated his position in March in his message to Congress titled "The Problems and Future of the Central City and Its Suburbs." "These problems are already in the front rank of national concern and interest," he observed. "They deserve to be in the front rank of government as well."

So again in 1965, another bill to elevate the HHFA to cabinet status was introduced in Congress. This time, the bill passed the House by a vote of 217 to 194, and the Senate by a 57 to 33 margin. On September 9, 1965, as President Johnson signed Public Law 80-174, he declared, "We are bringing into being today a very new and needed instrument to serve all the people of America." After more than a decade of debate and consensus building, annual legislative defeats, and five years of presidential endorsements, the Department of Housing and Urban Development was born.

Robert C. Weaver, the first secretary of HUD and the first black cabinet member, addresses a meeting of civic leaders in 1967. Weaver presided over the first three years of HUD's existence, from 1966 to 1968, and helped carry out several ground-breaking programs.

THREE

HUD's Growth and Development

Historically, the creation of new cabinet departments has been a slow process. The Department of the Interior was established after 33 years of discussion in the legislative and executive branches; for Agriculture the debate lasted 37 years; for Commerce, 39 years; and for Labor, more than 40 years. In comparison, the creation of HUD took a relatively short time from Representative Younger's original proposal for a Department of Urbiculture in 1954 to the signing of Public Law 80-174 in 1965. Still, the urgency of urban America's problems made this 11-year period seem like a very long delay. Congress's decision to embrace the creation of a department it formerly resisted was more than a simple change of heart.

HUD's Political Context

Obviously, a majority of senators and representatives did not wake up one morning in 1965 and finally decide that a Department of Housing and Urban Development might be a pretty good idea after all. Politics does not work that way. Rather, HUD, like all federal departments and agencies, was a creature of its political context. In other words, the political environment of the mid-1960s made the creation of HUD not only possible but also almost inevitable.

Of the important political conditions that precipitated the birth of HUD, the most immediate was the Democratic landslide victory in the 1964 elections. President Lyndon Johnson routed his Republican opponent, Senator Barry Goldwater of Arizona, returning to office with 61.6 percent of the popular vote and 486 of the 538 electoral votes. Goldwater carried only his native Arizona and five states in the Deep South. In addition, a large new group of liberal Democrats were elected to the House of Representatives—they "rode on Johnson's coattails" as the political saying goes. (The phrase refers to the phenomenon that occurs when the tremendous popularity of one candidate or unpopularity of another induces voters to vote the party line—to vote for *every* Democrat or *every* Republican on the ticket.) The sheer magnitude of this Democratic landslide facilitated the passage, in 1965, of the Johnson administration's Great Society legislative initiatives, such as civil rights reforms in a wide range of areas, the creation of the National Foundation on the Arts and the Humanities, and, of course, the establishment of HUD. It was not so much that members of Congress changed their mind about HUD; in many cases, the members themselves had changed. There were simply more newly elected Democrats in Congress who shared Johnson's goals.

The 1964 elections also coincided with a new development in American politics, a marked increase in the political power of the cities. The Supreme Court's decision in the 1962 case of *Baker v. Carr* mandated the reapportionment of state legislatures to reflect more accurately the population distribution among various areas of states. At around the same time, congressional districts were redrawn according to the results of the 1960 census. As cities became better represented in legislative bodies, urban interests began to wield more clout both in state capitals and in Washington, D.C. By the middle of the decade, the once rocky road to cabinet status for urban affairs was considerably smoother.

The 1964 election results underscored this development. For the first time since the post–Civil War Reconstruction era, the Deep South turned away from the Democratic party and supported the Republican candidate for president. The Democrats, their ties to the conservative, largely rural South now loosened (if not actually broken), were able to turn their attention more fully toward the needs of the cities.

Finally and perhaps most importantly, the early 1960s was a period of great racial ferment in the United States. A mass-based movement for civil rights

Throngs of reporters and elated backers crowd around civil rights leaders leaving the Capitol after the Senate approved the Civil Rights Act of 1964. The growing support for black civil rights had a profound effect on the creation of HUD and the direction of its programs.

was demanding that Congress and the White House move to outlaw racial discrimination in every sector of American life—education, voting, employment, housing, and transportation. Significant change, however, was slow in coming. Alongside the mainstream political strategy espoused by civil rights organizations such as the National Association for the Advancement of Colored People (NAACP) and leaders such as the Reverend Dr. Martin Luther King, Jr., groups advocating action outside the political process arose. These groups, such as the Black Panthers, urged a more militant response to oppression and discrimination. By 1964 and 1965, rising expectations within black communities collided with a frustrating reality, erupting in a wave of ghetto uprisings. In city after city, blacks vented their anger and disillusionment against a repressive white society and an unresponsive political system.

Faced with, on the one hand, an increasingly powerful and well-organized black political movement, and on the other hand, with the prospect of black

41

rebellion, liberal politicians were compelled to enact at least some reforms. The Civil Rights Act of 1964 and the Voting Rights Act of 1965 were passed in the hope of quelling this rising tide of black discontent. In addition, a large number of the blacks living in urban areas were concentrated by racial discrimination and low incomes into dilapidated, substandard housing. And so, the creation of HUD also should be seen as part of the Johnson administration's package of civil rights reforms.

Programs and Politics

The first major urban policy innovation after the creation of HUD was the Model Cities program. Enacted in 1966, the Model Cities program was designed to illustrate how poverty and blight in the nation's cities could be overcome if federal programs were coordinated in a way never previously attempted. It originally was to be called Demonstration Cities, but President Johnson felt that the term conjured up undesirable images of mass protest. "Look, this is 1965," he insisted half-humorously, "and we don't want any demonstrations in the cities!"

In the past, the federal government had attempted to deal with the problems of slum neighborhoods in a piecemeal manner, through a web of programs each concerned with one specific issue such as housing, education, health, or employment. A different agency administered each program and often carried on its own activities with little consideration of how the programs related to one another. At best, this approach could produce only limited results, for the beneficial effects of a single program would have little effect on the overall condition of the neighborhood. A new public housing project, for example, might provide better living conditions for a number of families but would do very little to improve the overall physical and social environment of the community.

Under the new Model Cities approach, the secretary of HUD would select a number of cities for participation in the program. Then the federal government would concentrate the full arsenal of its existing programs, covering the broadest range of issues, on certain target neighborhoods in these cities. This complex assortment of federal resources would be coordinated by a single authority, HUD. Perhaps the most daring component of this innovative program was the element of neighborhood participation; local residents were to have a voice in shaping and carrying out the programs in their own communities.

A local resident helps a Model Cities worker during an election for neighborhood representatives. The ambitious Model Cities program had mixed success, because local governments and community representatives often found themselves in bitter disagreement over goals and methods of development.

Model Cities was intended to correct the major flaws of the urban renewal program, which was created in 1949 to clear away slums and rebuild these blighted areas. Under this program, the people who were living in these targeted areas were supposed to be relocated to better neighborhoods. However, as President Johnson admitted in his message to Congress requesting passage for Model Cities, the human consequences of urban renewal were frequently overlooked: "The social and psychological effects of relocating the poor," he observed, "have not always been treated as what they are. They are the unavoidable consequences of slum clearance, demanding as much concern as physical redevelopment." Urban renewal cleared slums and then rebuilt the areas for a new class of users; the original inhabitants all too often were shuttled off to other slums. Model Cities would rebuild an entire slum neighborhood for the benefit of its present residents.

Despite its innovative approach and ambitious goals, Model Cities was less than a total success. Originally, the program was to have been introduced in just 150 communities across the nation. As progress in these initial model neighborhoods was demonstrated, the program would be expanded until it became the primary method of operation in every city. However, political reality conspired with the overly optimistic name of the program to spur on the premature expansion of Model Cities. Naturally, every mayor wanted to be the head of a "model city," and every member of Congress wanted a "model city" in his or her home district. The number of participating cities was increased, but the funding did not grow proportionately. In fact, the Nixon administration cut funding for Model Cities, in the dubious hope that private enterprise would take up the slack. It did not.

Further, the notion of citizen participation, although admirable in theory, proved unwieldy in practice. Model Cities generated intense power struggles both between local governments and neighborhood groups and within the neighborhood groups themselves. Because the stakes—real neighborhood improvement—were perceived as high, the level of acrimony was also high. In many cases, Model Cities created impasses and chaos, tearing apart neighborhoods it was supposed to bring together.

Finally, Model Cities stands as an example of the limits of a cabinet secretary's power. HUD was charged with coordinating the full range of existing programs that affect every aspect of urban life. However, these programs are managed by many different departments and agencies within the federal government. Bureaucracies jealously guard their administrative autonomy and precious budgetary resources and so are notoriously resistant to the kind of cooperation that Model Cities required. Personnel of agencies outside HUD did not want the HUD secretary telling them what to do.

Moreover, by law, the secretary of HUD could not, for example, increase funding for educational or health programs in a particular neighborhood, no matter how badly they were needed; those programs were handled by the Department of Health, Education, and Welfare. Model Cities gave HUD the authority to call on other departments for support, but the head of one cabinet department simply cannot issue orders to other departments. In sum, Model Cities was an ambitious but ultimately unworkable method for streamlining the implementation of urban policy.

In August 1968, President Johnson signed into law the Housing and Development Act of 1968. Never prone to understatement, he declared that this new law "can be the Magna Carta to liberate our cities." A far-reaching piece of legislation, it included provisions for expanding the production of government-owned low-rent housing, reconstructing decayed sections of cities, and facilitating the development of entirely new cities. The act's stated goal was the creation of 26 million units of new and rehabilitated housing in the next 10 years, with 6 million of these units to be built for the nation's ill-housed.

The law's Section 235 program was designed to bring homeownership within the reach of more than 1 million low-income families by 1978. An eligible family would pay 20 percent of its income toward the cost of financing its home purchase, and the federal government would make up the rest. The amount of

(continued on page 48)

The Taino Towers apartment complex (foreground) in Manhattan was built under the provisions of Section 236, part of the Housing and Development Act of 1968. During the 4 years that sections 236 and 235 of the 1968 act were in effect, more than 1.5 million units of subsidized housing were produced.

The Promise—and Failure— of Urban Renewal

In addition to expanding federal involvement in public housing, the Housing Act of 1949 established a program of large-scale slum clearance that became known as urban renewal. The federal government provided local agencies with funding as well as the power of eminent domain (the right to appropriate private property for public use, with payment to the owner). The local agency used this money and power to condemn slum neighborhoods, tear down the buildings, and then resell the land to private developers. Slum dwellers would be relocated to "decent, safe, and sanitary" housing, as the act mandated.

Urban renewal was intended to stimulate large-scale private rebuilding, revitalize the cities' downtown areas, and add new revenues to dwindling municipal tax coffers. The program did produce real benefits. Blight and deterioration were dramatically reduced in hundreds of cities. Large stretches of downtown areas were reborn, as slums gave way to office towers, shopping centers, modern apartment buildings, and cultural complexes. Still, urban renewal was anything but a total success.

The flaw in the urban renewal program was summed up best by sociologist Herbert J. Gans: "It is a method for eliminating the slums in order to 'renew' the city, rather than a program for properly rehousing slum dwellers." The question many inner-city dwellers and advocates angrily asked—"renewal for whom?"—was a fair one. Between 1949 and 1967, for example, the urban renewal program forced 400,000 low- and moderate-income families from their homes; urban renewal produced new housing for only 40,000 families.

In the program's first 15 years (1949–64), only one-half of 1 percent of all federal urban renewal expenditures was spent on the relocation of dispossessed slum dwellers to "decent, safe, and sanitary" housing. The local renewal agencies, which were supposed to take care of relocation, were largely frustrated—in most cities, vacant, low-cost, standard quality housing is in extremely short supply, if available at all. A 1961 study of renewal projects in 41 cities showed that 60 percent of the tenants who were dispossessed were merely moved to other slums. By pushing relocated families into old buildings that then became overcrowded and subsequently deteriorated, renewal created new slums and made old ones worse.

Urban renewal destroyed entire neighborhoods, uprooting long-term residents, closing down their social and cultural institutions, bankrupting their businesses, scattering families and friends. In many cases black neighborhoods were obliterated, which prompted the often-heard

In the early 1960s before urban renewal, the area behind historic Independence Hall in Philadelphia was a jumble of aging, four-story row houses, dilapidated factories, and narrow streets.

After urban renewal, a 1967 photograph reveals a mall stretching behind Independence Hall and a modern new office building rising on the left. However, the design included no housing.

charge, "Urban renewal is Negro removal." Urban renewal may have helped to intensify the black resentment and anger that erupted in the ghetto rebellions of the 1960s.

By the 1960s, urban renewal had come under attack both from liberals, who were disappointed by its unkept promises, and conservatives, who seized on it as yet another costly failure of "big government." Perhaps urban renewal could have been salvaged if policymakers changed its focus and made it into

what it claimed to be, but in fact, never was—an urban rehousing program. That never happened. In 1973, President Nixon curtailed a number of federal housing programs, ending urban renewal. Urban renewal failed the urban poor not because it did not achieve its primary goals—slum clearance and downtown redevelopment—but because in accomplishing these things, it treated the critical housing needs of the poor as an unimportant, secondary concern.

47

(continued from page 45)

interest the family would have to pay on the mortgage was reduced, under this program, to just 1 percent. By August 1970, 2 years after the program went into effect, nearly 110,000 houses were already occupied or were being constructed under Section 235. The law also created the Section 236 program, a similar subsidy for the production of rental housing. The 1968 act gave the housing industry a tremendous boost, and housing production in the United States was never higher. From 1968 through 1972, 1,665,550 units of subsidized housing were produced, more than in the previous 30 years.

During the Nixon administration's first four years (1969–73), HUD secretary George Romney, a former governor of Michigan, presided over this housing surge, a product of the policies of the Johnson administration. By 1972, federal assistance programs accounted for 25 percent of all housing starts. Romney, who cared deeply about the cities, argued for increased public housing and urged Nixon to continue the Model Cities program.

As time passed, however, it became clear that Romney and HUD were pursuing goals outside the main concerns of the Nixon administration. Trusted cronies of Nixon, such as Attorney General John Mitchell and chief domestic affairs adviser John Ehrlichman, had the president's ear and promoted a more conservative, less active agenda. Romney's influence with the White House dwindled to nothing, and so he resigned the cabinet in December 1972, pending Senate approval of his replacement.

That same month, rumors began to circulate within HUD and throughout Washington that Nixon was considering a *moratorium*, or total freeze, on housing programs. HUD area offices frantically processed applications for Sections 235 and 236 subsidies in fear that the rumors might be true. These suspicions were well founded. In one of his last acts as HUD secretary, Romney, who had served as the federal government's general in the war against slums, was ordered by his commander in chief to surrender.

On January 8, 1973, in a speech before the convention of the National Association of Home Builders, Romney announced a freeze on urban renewal, Model Cities, and all subsidized housing programs, including Sections 235 and 236. A few months later, Nixon's nominee as HUD secretary, James Lynn, explained to a House committee that the moratorium was instituted because of "mounting evidence that the present program structure we now have cannot yield effective results." In other words, the administration decreed the entire apparatus of federal housing policy to be a complete and irredeemable failure. In response to this action, a coalition of 49 organizations, including the National Association of Home Builders, the National League of Cities, the Mortgage

48

Secretary George Romney directed HUD through some of its most active years, from 1969 to 1972. When President Nixon made his opposition to federal housing programs clear, Romney resigned, but Nixon first forced him to announce an across-the-board freeze on public-housing assistance, Model Cities, and urban renewal.

Bankers Association, and the nation's most powerful union, the American Federation of Labor and Congress of Industrial Organizations (the AFL-CIO), called on Congress to delay confirmation of Lynn and other Nixon appointees until the freeze was lifted. However, through the next 18 months, every congressional attempt to force Nixon to cancel the ban met with failure.

At the time of the moratorium, the administration directed HUD to conduct a study of the frozen programs. Thirteen months later, the report, *Housing in the Seventies*, was released. The controversial document maintained that the suspended programs were inequitable, inefficient, and impractical. A nonpartisan analysis of the study conducted by the Congressional Research Service in the Library of Congress exposed faulty reasoning, numerous errors of fact, and distortions of the language of the laws and congressional reports throughout *Housing in the Seventies*. Senator John Sparkman of Alabama charged that the HUD report "was hastily written . . . to support the already announced opposition to the kinds of housing subsidies which the Nixon administration had inherited and administered for four years." The report also was designed to justify a proposed new approach to addressing the housing problems of the poor—housing allowances.

Nixon argued that previous housing subsidy programs were flawed because they attempted to treat the symptom—poor housing—instead of the disease—poverty. These programs, he maintained, "have been helping the builders directly and the poor only indirectly." So, under his proposed housing allowance program, the government, instead of providing the poor with a place to live, would provide them with a direct cash payment. This subsidy would allow low-income families to purchase rental housing on the private market, housing that they otherwise would not have been able to afford. "This plan," Nixon declared, "would give the poor the freedom and responsibility to make their own choice about housing." The idea was not new; similar schemes had been studied and rejected in 1937, 1948, and 1953. Congress did the same to Nixon's plan.

By the summer of 1974, as the Watergate scandal enveloped Nixon's administration and the threat of impeachment loomed over the president, a beleaguered Nixon needed whatever congressional goodwill he could get. He rescinded the moratorium on housing subsidies and backed a HUD-inspired community development bill that Congress passed as the Housing and Community Development Act of 1974. Exactly one week after Nixon resigned the presidency, the bill was signed into law by his successor, Gerald Ford.

This comprehensive new law provided for various forms of housing rehabilitation, apartment subsidies, and mortgage interest subsidies. Under the act's rent supplement provision, Section 8, the amount of rent that a tenant can afford is calculated as a percentage of the tenant's income. The federal government pays the landlord the difference between that amount and the fair market rent of the unit.

Most significantly, the 1974 act eliminated or absorbed seven existing *categorical grant* programs. The funds in a categorical grant are earmarked for specific purposes only, including urban renewal and Model Cities. These grants were incorporated into a new block grant structure. Block grants are federal funds that may be used for unspecified purposes within a general area, such as

President Ford signs the Housing and Community Development Act of 1974. The HUD-backed bill authorized rent supplements, housing rehabilitation, mortgage interest subsidies, and a new system of block grants to communities for development.

education or, in this case, urban improvement. The secretary of HUD was authorized to distribute these community development block grants (CDBGs) to state and local governments. Each locality was allowed considerable freedom in choosing how to use its CDBG.

In the original Nixon administration proposal, these local community development programs were not subject to review by HUD. Congress found this unacceptable, but the final law still required far less federal oversight than ever before. Under Nixon, and then Ford, HUD reduced itself to little more than a rubber stamp for the wishes of local government. The block grant system cut

51

bureaucratic red tape and transferred decision-making authority to those closest to the problems. However, critics argued that it vested too much power in local governments, which are prone to the influence of the most powerful—and the least needy—special interests.

By the start of the Carter administration (1977–81), the optimism of the early 1960s had faded, replaced by gloomy perceptions of economic stagnation, concern over budget deficits, and the belief that government and society must accept limits on what they can accomplish. Government, in the eyes of many people, had grown too large, too powerful, and most importantly, too expensive. Compared with previous Democratic administrations, the Carter White House exhibited little enthusiasm for new and costly social welfare programs. Overall, the political and economic climate had shifted in a more conservative direction.

Carter's only major urban policy initiative was the Urban Development Action Grant (UDAG) program. This program supported large redevelopment projects in economically distressed cities. These ventures, which went beyond the scope of CDBGs, received federal funding because they could increase a city's tax base and employment rate. Reflecting the cautious tone of the times, the program required that, in order to receive a UDAG, a city must secure private investment at a level greater than the government's commitment. Between 1977 and 1981, UDAGs contributed $500 million to urban development in the United States.

The Carter administration was ambivalent and unenthusiastic in its support for HUD; the subsequent Reagan administration (1981–89) was, from the start, committed to a full-scale reduction of the department and its programs. Beginning with fiscal year 1982, Reagan's director of the Office of Management and Budget (OMB), David Stockman, instituted deep cuts in HUD's budget. One of the new administration's goals was to end, or at least severely curtail, construction of low-cost public housing. During the Carter presidency, the federal government funded about 40,000 such units annually, a figure that dropped to 5,000 under Reagan. From fiscal years 1981 through 1989, federal spending on subsidized housing declined by 82 percent, or $34 billion, allowing for inflation. Housing subsidy programs, such as Section 8, CDBGs, and UDAGs also were reduced substantially.

Alongside these drastic budget reductions, Congress, at the White House's insistence, enacted a program of "housing vouchers" on an experimental basis in 1983; it became permanent in 1987. The program, which is similar to Nixon's housing allowance proposal, provides low-income families with a direct cash supplement so that they can purchase improved housing on the open market.

A Community Development Block Grant (CDBG), allocated by HUD to Richmond, Virginia, helped finance the rehabilitation of this old theater. It became the Virginia Center for the Performing Arts.

Women work at the Berlin Steel Plant in Baltimore, Maryland, a project financed partially by an Urban Development Action Grant (UDAG) from HUD and partially by private investment. President Carter instituted UDAGs in 1977; in 1982, President Reagan severely curtailed them as well as all other HUD funding programs.

The administration insisted that housing vouchers would eliminate the need for the federal government to construct new subsidized housing units and that they would provide the poor with greater freedom of choice in selecting where to live. Critics charged that housing vouchers were merely a smoke screen created to hide the administration's attack on the existing federal housing programs. Housing vouchers reflected the conservative ideology of the Reagan era, which was dedicated to reducing the role of government and promoting the mechanisms of the free market. And so, like each of its predecessors, the Reagan administration put its political stamp on HUD and its programs.

HUD was a product of the liberal political climate of the mid-1960s; many of its programs are designed to benefit the urban poor, a large portion of whom are black. Over the two and a half decades since its creation, this perception of HUD as the embodiment of liberal and black (as well as, of course, urban) interests has been both influential and persistent. Democrats have promoted the establishment and expansion of HUD and its programs to help keep the support of groups important to their party's traditional electoral coalition—northern, urban, and black voters. Republicans, for their part, have advocated the curtailing of HUD's activities to appeal to conservative and rural voters and to hasten the erosion of white southern support from the Democrats. Like all other departments and agencies within the executive branch, the policies, the programs, and the very existence of HUD have been shaped by political forces—in particular, by the special dynamics of presidential politics.

At HUD headquarters, Seventh and E streets, SW, in Washington, D.C.,
HUD administrators set departmental policy, priorities, and procedures and
direct the activities of regional and field offices.

FOUR

The Structure of HUD

Who works at HUD and what do they do? Understanding the answers to these questions gives a clear picture of the department and how it is organized.

The HUD staff falls into four general employment categories. *Executive level* employees are appointed by the president and confirmed by the Senate. HUD has 11 executive level appointees—the secretary, the under secretary, the general counsel, and the 8 assistant secretaries.

Senior Executive Service (SES) jobs are high-level management and policy-making positions. The Office of Personnel Management (OPM) determines the SES allocation for each department and agency in the executive branch. HUD has 120 SES positions, of which 30 are designated as noncareer posts. Appointees to noncareer positions are chosen by the secretary and must be cleared by the White House. Appointees in career positions are selected through a competitive process that includes approval of their qualifications by the OPM.

Excepted Service jobs are those positions that are below SES level and exempted from the competitive appointment process. They include professionals, such as attorneys, and certain policy-making and confidential jobs referred to as "Schedule C" positions. Experts and consultants are also in the Excepted

Service category and are paid only for the days they actually work for the department.

All other jobs fall under the heading of *Competitive Service*. These are the well-known civil service positions, filled by the best-qualified applicants according to competitive testing procedures established by the OPM.

Departmental Organization

HUD is administered by the *secretary*, who is responsible for the management of all of the department's programs and functions. A secretary is nominated by the president and must be confirmed by the Senate, as other executive-level employees are. The secretary advises the president on federal policy, programs, and activities in the areas of housing and community development. The secretary also formulates HUD's legislative program and makes policy recommendations to the president that may be incorporated in the annual State of the Union message and the proposed federal budget.

In addition, the HUD secretary is responsible for overseeing the operations of the secondary mortgage market. This market exists because the government created several institutions that purchase mortgages from lenders in order to provide funds for the loan industry. The secretary sets the policies, directs the administration, and appoints the officers of the Government National Mortgage Association, a government corporation within the department. The HUD secretary also has regulatory authority over the privately owned Federal National Mortgage Association.

As the federal government's chief advocate in the fields of housing and community development, the HUD secretary attempts to enlist the cooperation of private enterprise in achieving the objectives of the department. The secretary promotes urban growth and the efficient use of housing and community development resources by stimulating private sector ventures and public-private sector partnerships. Through the leadership of the HUD secretary, private enterprise is encouraged to serve as large a part of the nation's total housing and community needs as possible.

Finally, the secretary acts as the federal government's liaison on housing and urban development matters, assisting the president in achieving maximum coordination in these areas among the various levels of government. In this capacity, the secretary confers with governors and other state officials, as well as with regional and local governmental leaders. The secretary also interprets

The Federal National Mortgage Association (Fannie Mae), housed in a building separate from HUD headquarters, is a privately owned corporation. Because Fannie Mae deals with the buying and selling of home mortgages, however, the HUD secretary has regulatory authority over the company.

federal programs to organizations and officials representing builders and other facets of the housing industry, banks and other lending institutions, labor unions, minority groups, public interest groups, and social service organizations.

The *under secretary* helps the secretary carry out these duties and responsibilities and serves as acting secretary should the secretary be absent or become disabled. The office of the secretary also contains a number of *staff offices* that have responsibility in the following specialized areas: international affairs, labor relations, small and disadvantaged business utilization, and Indian and Alaskan native programs. In addition, the department's staff offices include the Administrative Law Judge and the HUD Board of Contract Appeals.

Each of HUD's eight *assistant secretaries* is responsible for a specific program area (such as public and Indian housing, or community planning and development) or a support function (such as legislation and congressional relations, policy research and development, or public affairs). The *general counsel* provides the HUD secretary and staff with legal opinions and services with respect to HUD's programs and activities and assists in the development of legislation. Two *deputy under secretaries* advise the department on matters concerning field coordination (the management of HUD's regional and field offices) and intergovernmental relations.

There are three levels of organization in HUD. Located in Washington, D.C., HUD *headquarters* sets departmental policy, priorities, and procedures; directs, monitors, and evaluates the administration of programs by the regional and field offices; and allocates funds and staffing for the regions. Headquarters conducts formal evaluation reviews of the regional offices to assess the management and performance of HUD's programs and to ensure that these offices comply with departmental policy and procedures.

HUD headquarters is housed in a 10-story building located at Seventh and E streets, SW, in Washington, D.C. Ground was broken on August 3, 1965, and the finished structure, which covers three-quarters of a city block and cost $26 million, was dedicated by President Johnson on September 8, 1968. Constructed in a double-Y shape, its gracefully curving, symmetrical design represents a departure from the usual block or wing configurations of most federal office buildings.

Each of HUD's 10 *regional offices* is headed by a regional administrator–regional housing commissioner (RA), who is responsible for managing the department's programs and satisfying its goals and objectives within the immediate geographic area. The RA directs and evaluates the performance of the field offices within the region and allocates funds and staffing among those offices.

Each region is broken down into several *field offices*, which supervise and direct specific, assigned programs. There are 71 HUD field offices, designated according to 1 of 4 categories:

- The 30 *Category A offices* are responsible for the full range of HUD programs—housing, public housing, community planning and development, and fair housing and equal opportunity—within their geographic areas.
- The 11 *Category B offices* are responsible only for single-family and multi-family housing programs.
- The 22 *Category C offices* are limited to all activities concerning home mortgage insurance programs.
- The eight *Category D offices* are limited to home mortgage insurance application processing only.

All field office managers in Categories A, B, and C are appointed by the secretary of HUD and are accountable to the RA; Category D offices are headed by a chief who is appointed by the RA and reports to the director of housing development in the regional office. The category designations A through D were created for internal HUD use only. In external correspondence and dealings, field offices are referred to by the name of the city in which they are located.

Oversight

The Office of the Inspector General (OIG) is an independent office within HUD responsible for detecting and investigating waste, fraud, and abuse in the department. The OIG's investigative authority extends to the practices of contractors, recipients of HUD grants, and other parties involved in carrying out HUD programs. The OIG conducts audits to determine the proper conduct of financial operations and the efficient use of resources. When necessary, it also conducts criminal inquiries. The office also serves as a liaison on audits and other investigative matters with such agencies as the General Accounting Office (GAO), the Department of Justice, and the President's Council on Integrity and Efficiency. Its staff, in headquarters and the field, totals about 500.

Within the executive branch there are three major offices that oversee all or part of the operations of the various federal departments, including HUD. The OMB examines each major component of HUD's budget and gives final approval to its funding and staffing request before it is submitted to Congress each year. The OMB also reviews and approves proposed departmental regulations, policies, and legislation and monitors compliance with plans designed to improve the management of government. The OPM oversees HUD's personnel policies and operations and issues regulations regarding the department's staffing and other personnel-related activities. The General Services Administration (GSA) manages the federal government's real property assets, such as the HUD building, oversees the acquisition of supplies and the use of government vehicles, and develops policies on government travel.

Within the legislative branch, a large number of offices and committees oversee, either directly or indirectly, the operations of HUD. The Congressional Budget Office (CBO), an arm of the Senate and House Budget committees, analyzes the economic impact of government programs. As such, it is a vital source of information for the development of congressional budget estimates for the executive agencies and departments, including HUD. The GAO evaluates the efficiency, economy, and effectiveness of all government activities. The GAO continually audits HUD programs and procedures.

Most of HUD's authorizing legislation is handled by the Senate Committee on Banking, Housing, and Urban Affairs (through its Subcommittee on Housing and Urban Affairs) and the House Committee on Banking, Finance, and Urban Affairs (through its Subcommittee on Housing and Community Development). The department must present its proposals for changes in existing legislation and requests for the enactment of new legislation to these committees. The Senate and House Budget committees examine HUD's funding levels, program descriptions, and program accomplishments in order to establish the department's annual budget target. The Senate and House Appropriations committees (through their respective subcommittees on HUD-Independent Agencies) approve HUD's funding and staffing levels for each fiscal year.

A number of other congressional committees are involved with specific aspects of HUD's activities. For example, the Senate and House Judiciary committees are concerned with Title VII (Fair Housing) of the Civil Rights Act of 1968, and all other civil rights laws that affect HUD's programs. The Senate Special Committee on Aging and the House Select Committee on Aging (Subcommittee on Housing and Consumer Interest) pay particular attention to HUD's housing programs for senior citizens. The Joint Economic Committee is

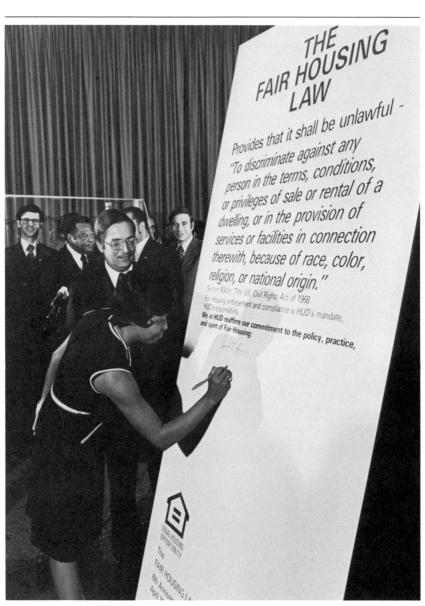

THE
FAIR HOUSING
LAW

Provides that it shall be unlawful –
"To discriminate against any
person in the terms, conditions,
or privileges of sale or rental of a
dwelling, or in the provision of
services or facilities in connection
therewith, because of race, color,
religion, or national origin."
Section 804(b), Title VIII, Civil Rights Act of 1968
Fair Housing enforcement and compliance is HUD's mandate,
HUD's responsibility.
We at HUD reaffirm our commitment to the policy, practice,
and spirit of Fair Housing:

EQUAL HOUSING
OPPORTUNITY
The
FAIR HOUSING
6th Anniver...
April 1...

HUD staffers sign a poster at a celebration of the 6th anniversary of the Civil Rights Act of 1968. As the sign notes, HUD is responsible for enforcing the fair-housing provisions of the act throughout the full range of its housing programs.

63

Seymour Smith (left), an elder of the Maidu Indians in northern California, looks on as federal staffers from HUD and the Farmers Home Administration (FmHA) check the rehabilitation of his home. HUD works with several other agencies to assist Native American housing efforts in rural areas.

involved in matters pertaining to the housing and mortgage markets and their relationships with economic planning. The Senate Select Committee on Indian Affairs and the House Committee on Interior and Insular Affairs oversee policies that affect the welfare of Native Americans, including HUD's Indian housing programs.

Related Organizations

The Department of Veterans Affairs (VA) administers a home loan program for members and veterans of the armed forces that is generally similar to the FHA's single-family mortgage insurance program, which is administered by

HUD. The Farmers Home Administration (FmHA) within the Department of Agriculture functions as a lender of last resort for low- and moderate-income borrowers in rural areas. For an area to be eligible for FmHA assistance, the secretaries of agriculture and HUD must determine that it suffers from a serious lack of mortgage credit.

Located in the HUD headquarters building, the Interagency Council for the Homeless reviews and coordinates federal programs and activities designed to help the homeless. The council works with state and local governments on homeless-related efforts, and collects and disseminates information on activities concerning homelessness. Created in 1987, its members are the heads of 10 cabinet departments and 5 independent agencies.

HUD staffers gather beneath a huge banner decorating the outside of HUD headquarters. The banner proclaims HUD's dedication to fair housing—a commitment that was increasingly hard to fulfill throughout the 1980s because of budget cuts and mismanagement at the department.

FIVE

HUD's Programs and Functions

The programs of the Department of Housing and Urban Development cover four major areas: housing financing, public and Indian housing, community planning and development, and fair housing and equal opportunity. In addition, a number of offices within the department handle a range of important support functions. In most cases an assistant secretary has responsibility for a particular program area or function.

Housing Financing

The *assistant secretary for housing–federal housing commissioner* directs the housing programs and functions of HUD. This office within HUD supports the production, financing, and management of new and substantially rehabilitated housing, and the conservation and preservation of the existing housing stock.

The assistant secretary for housing–federal housing commissioner administers the approximately 40 mortgage and loan programs of the Federal Housing Administration (FHA). Created in 1934 to aid families distressed by the depression, as well as to reinvigorate the comatose housing industry, the FHA was incorporated into HUD when the department was established in 1965. Its programs provide insurance to lenders in order to encourage them to make loans to first-time buyers and other borrowers who might not qualify for conventional mortgages. Because its programs alleviate the risk in what otherwise would be considered high-risk loans, FHA programs stimulate the flow of mortgage funds and make homeownership possible for a greatly increased number of families.

Prospective homeowners who wish to participate in the FHA's single-family mortgage insurance program must apply to a HUD-approved lender, who in turn applies to HUD. The interest rates of FHA loans are the same as the rates for conventional loans, but down payment requirements are lower. If a borrower defaults on an FHA-insured loan, the mortgage company can file an insurance claim with HUD in the amount of the yet unpaid portion of the loan. The department will pay the claim and become the owner of the property. HUD's Property Disposition staff and its contractors manage and maintain these houses, renting them or, if possible, reselling them to new owners. The mortgages of approximately 7 million American homeowners are insured under the FHA's single-family mortgage insurance programs. The FHA also insures loans to developers and builders who are constructing or rehabilitating apartments and other multifamily housing projects, and loans made by lenders to people who want to make improvements on their homes or buy mobile homes.

The assistant secretary for housing also administers the Section 202 program, under which the government provides direct, 40-year loans to help private, nonprofit corporations and consumer cooperatives finance the construction or rehabilitation of housing for senior citizens or the handicapped. The assistant secretary also handles the three Section 8 programs: the Housing Certificate and Housing Voucher programs, which provide rental assistance to low-income families, and the Moderate Rehabilitation program, which compensates owners of rental housing for the costs incurred in improving and rehabilitating these units. Finally, the assistant secretary serves as chair of the Mortgagee Review Board, which is authorized to withdraw mortgage approvals; the board's decisions are subject to appeal and review by the HUD Board of Contract Appeals.

By guaranteeing the securities, such as bonds, that are issued and sold by private lending institutions, HUD's *Government National Mortgage Association* (GNMA, popularly known as Ginnie Mae) helps convert investment capital into home mortgages. These high-yield, no-risk, government-guaranteed securities attract funds into the mortgage market that otherwise might not be available, and so, provide the financing for most FHA (as well as VA and FmHA) home

Luther Towers is an apartment complex specifically designed for senior citizens and physically challenged residents in Wilmington, Delaware. The building was financed with the aid of HUD's Section 202 program, which allows HUD to make direct, 40-year loans to help private nonprofit corporations and consumer cooperatives build or refurbish such facilities.

loans. During periods of credit shortages, these funds may become virtually the only source of mortgage money available. Supported by the full faith and credit of the United States government, GNMA-backed securities are highly desirable investments and the most widely held and traded mortgage instruments in the world.

Unlike the GNMA, the *Federal National Mortgage Association* (FNMA, popularly known as Fannie Mae) is not a part of HUD, or even the government. Although it was created in 1938 as an independent federal agency, in 1968 the FNMA was made a private corporation operating under the guidance of the HUD secretary. The FNMA buys and sells mortgages, including those insured by the FHA, after the mortgages have been made by a private lender, in what is called the "secondary mortgage market." This gives the officers of a lending institution an incentive to make mortgage loans, because they know that, if the institution should need cash, they can sell the mortgages to the FNMA. And so, in the language of finance, FHA-insured loans are liquid investments—that is, they can be converted easily into cash, a highly valued characteristic.

Public and Indian Housing

The *assistant secretary for public and Indian housing* administers all of the federal government's public and Indian housing programs. The approximately 1.4 million units of federally subsidized rental housing in the United States are managed by 3,000 local public and Indian housing agencies.

HUD's public housing program provides public housing agencies (PHAs) of local governments with technical and financial assistance in planning, developing, and managing rental housing for low-income families. There are three main forms of federal financial aid: funding for the costs of developing and constructing new public housing projects, annual contributions toward the operating costs of existing projects, and modernization funds for the upgrading and improvement of public housing. Because the federal government subsidizes the cost of public housing, local PHAs can keep rents at a level that low-income families can afford.

In its basic structure, HUD's Indian housing program is similar to its public housing program. Federal assistance enables local Indian housing authorities (IHAs) to provide affordable rental housing for low-income Indians and Alaskan natives. In addition, the department's Indian Mutual-Help Homeownership

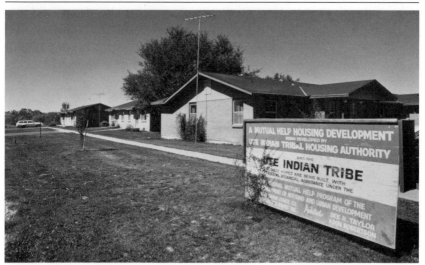

A sign marks this development in Utah as part of HUD's Indian Mutual Help Homeownership Opportunity program. The Ute Indians in this project, and others like it, can rent their homes for a time and eventually purchase them.

Shoppers stroll through the Albee Square Mall in Brooklyn, New York, in 1982. The mall was developed with money provided by a UDAG, a grant that requires financial investment by private companies. Although this grant did not go toward housing construction, it did enable the construction of a commercial project that provides jobs and increased tax revenues in a distressed neighborhood.

Opportunity program offers a lease-purchase arrangement under which the occupants of some rental projects, over time, can acquire ownership of their homes.

Community Planning and Development

The *assistant secretary for community planning and development* administers the grant programs through which HUD provides funds to states and communities for a number of activities, such as solving community development problems, providing homeless shelters, restoring neighborhoods, and fostering local job creation and economic development.

Established in 1974, the community development block grants (CDBGs) constitute the bulk of HUD's grant activity. About 70 percent of HUD's block grant money is used for *entitlement grants*. By law, cities with populations of more than 50,000 and urban counties with populations of more than 200,000 are entitled to an annual grant. Nonentitlement grants make up the other 30 percent of CDBG funds. These are allocated among states, which in turn award grants to smaller communities according to a formula based on such factors as comparative levels of population, poverty, housing overcrowding, the age of housing, and stagnant growth.

CDBGs may be used to carry out a wide range of activities directed at economic development, neighborhood revitalization, and the provision of improved facilities and services. Recipients enjoy·wide latitude in using their block grant funds. However, the law stipulates that during the first 3 years that a grant is received, at least 60 percent of the resources must be used to benefit low- and moderate-income persons. Some of the specific activities that can be carried out with CDBG funds include the following: acquisition of real property, rehabilitation of residential and nonresidential structures, provisions for public improvements (such as water or sewer facilities, streets, or neighborhood centers), and energy conservation.

The Urban Development Action Grant (UDAG) program, enacted in 1977, was designed to stimulate private investment in commercial or industrial projects, thus creating new, permanent jobs and increasing tax revenues in severely distressed urban areas. Cities receiving UDAG funds must secure a private investment of at least $2.50 for every federal dollar spent. Unlike CDBGs, these grants are awarded through an application process in which communities compete with one another for funding. From 1977 to 1988, the UDAG program funded nearly 3,000 projects with a total price tag of $4.7 billion. No new UDAG funds were appropriated for fiscal year 1989.

The assistant secretary for community planning and development also administers HUD's Urban Homesteading program. Under this program, unoccupied homes that, because of foreclosures, are owned by HUD, the VA, and the FmHA are transferred to local agencies. These agencies, in turn, transfer the properties at little or no cost to families who agree to live in them for at least five years and bring them up to housing codes. The families may receive low-interest loans to assist them in their rehabilitation efforts.

The Secretary's Discretionary Fund consists of money to be used for special projects and technical assistance awards to help implement the various programs authorized by Title I of the 1974 Housing and Community Development Act. (Title I of the act instituted CDBGs.) In 1989, this fund disbursed approximately $50 million to special constituencies—areas that are not eligible for entitlement grants or nonentitlement grants, such as Guam, the U.S. Virgin Islands, and Samoa—and to Indian tribes and groups of Alaskan natives. The secretary can also direct that money be paid from this fund to state and local governments and to area community planning groups that their governments indicate can help them with technical assistance in community planning activities. Such advisory groups include semiprivate groups that may

The glass panes of a greenhouse on a smartly refurbished brick home in downtown Baltimore stand in sharp contrast to a debris-strewn lot next door. The house was renovated under HUD's Urban Homesteading program, which awards loans and eventual ownership to families who fix up houses in run-down neighborhoods.

be considered overqualified for receiving funds according to HUD guidelines but in the secretary's or local government's view can provide necessary technical assistance unavailable elsewhere.

Enacted in 1987 as the brainchild of the Reagan administration, the Federal Enterprise Zone program was designed to encourage job creation and entrepreneurship in distressed inner cities and rural areas. The HUD secretary may designate up to 100 such zones nationwide in which HUD's regulations are waived, thereby speeding up the delivery of its programs. Private firms engaged in economic development within these zones are granted relief from federal regulations and taxes.

Emergency shelter grants assist larger cities in renovating, rehabilitating, or converting buildings for use as emergency shelters for the homeless. These funds also may be spent on essential services for the homeless and operating costs, such as insurance, maintenance, utilities, and furnishings.

Fair Housing and Equal Opportunity

The *assistant secretary for fair housing and equal opportunity* (FHEO) investigates and prosecutes housing discrimination complaints under Title VII of the Civil Rights Act of 1968, which prohibits discrimination in housing on the basis of race, color, religion, sex, or national origin. In addition, the FHEO enforces accessibility for handicapped persons in federally assisted programs, advises the secretary on issues and policies affecting civil rights and equal opportunity in the areas of housing and community development, and ensures affirmative action and equal employment opportunity within the department. The Fair Housing Amendments Act of 1988 strengthened enforcement procedures and added the handicapped and families with children to the list of groups that are protected against housing discrimination. The Fair Housing Initiatives program, implemented in 1989, provides funding to public and private groups that are involved in fighting or eliminating discriminatory housing practices.

Program Support Functions

The *assistant secretary for policy development and research* (PD&R) conducts evaluations of existing HUD programs, develops and assesses the impact of alternative proposals for new policies and programs, carries out research on building technology and housing quality, and collects and analyzes data on housing markets. The PD&R produces monthly reports on housing starts, the biennial *President's National Urban Policy Report*, and annual reports on the Federal National Mortgage Association.

The *assistant secretary for legislation and congressional relations* (LCR) works with HUD's Office of the General Counsel (OGC) and the various program offices to develop the department's position on legislative matters. The assistant secretary oversees the progress of HUD's legislative and appropriations initiatives in Congress and ensures that all testimony and responses to congressional inquiries are consistent with the secretary's positions. The office also helps resolve differences with the Office of Management and Budget on legislative issues.

The *OGC* is the primary legal adviser to the secretary and staff on matters pertaining to the development and implementation of HUD's programs, policies, and activities. Among the duties of this office are preparing the department's annual program of authorization legislation, reviewing and clearing testimony before congressional hearings, drafting and clearing regulations, and preparing the department's views on proposed executive orders.

The *assistant secretary for administration* directs the administrative management of the department; plans and implements the distribution and use of HUD's personnel, equipment, and material; and develops and executes management policies and procedures for HUD headquarters and its regional and field offices. The assistant secretary provides support services to the department in such areas as personnel and training, budget, finance and accounting, procurement and contracting, and computer support. The assistant secretary also acts as HUD's liaison with the OMB, the OPM, the GSA, and the House and Senate Appropriations committees.

The post of the *deputy under secretary for field coordination* is part of the office of the secretary of the department. This deputy under secretary keeps the HUD secretary and staff informed about the effectiveness of regional and field operating policies and procedures and serves as the principal point of communication between the secretary and the regional and field offices.

The *deputy under secretary for intergovernmental relations* advises the secretary on policy matters that affect other levels of government. The holder of this office is the department's main contact point with state and local governments and public and private interest groups.

Public Affairs

The *assistant secretary for public affairs* is HUD's focal point for all matters relating to public information and communication with the media. This office responds to inquiries received from the public and the press; prepares press releases, statements, speeches, testimony, and other briefing materials for the secretary; schedules the secretary's public appearances; and arranges news media contact for other senior HUD officials.

Other Support Functions

Within the office of the HUD secretary, a number of offices and assistants perform vital program and administrative support functions. The *special assistant for Indian and Alaska native housing* ensures that the unique housing and community development needs of Indians and Alaskan natives are addressed in HUD's policies and programs. The *Office of Small and Disadvan-*

The HUD office of the special assistant for Indian and Alaska native housing pays particular attention to Indian housing needs, and the Office of Small and Disadvantaged Business Utilization ensures that minority-owned or -run companies get business from the department. A photograph of an Indian worker at a HUD-funded Indian housing project in Minnesota shows how the two offices can cooperate.

taged Business Utilization oversees the department's contracting activities, making certain that small businesses, as well as black-, women-, and other minority-owned businesses, participate in HUD projects.

The *assistant to the secretary for labor relations* enforces labor standards in HUD-assisted construction activities and oversees the wage system for maintenance workers who are employed by local housing agencies in HUD-subsidized public housing projects. The *assistant to the secretary for international affairs* supports the department's participation in international programs related to urban affairs and building construction technology. The *special assistant to the secretary–director of executive secretariat* is the central coordinating officer for all secretarial correspondence.

The *HUD Board of Contract Appeals* is the department's independent forum in which contractors may appeal decisions by HUD officials. The board has the power to decide appeals concerning the awarding of grants, the exclusion and suspension of contractors from HUD activities, decisions of the Mortgagee Review Board, and the withholding of tax refunds of people who are indebted to the department. The board has the flexibility to conduct either a full trial with formal trial procedures or more informal, expedited hearings for appellants with small claims against the department. More than half of the board's hearings are held in the appellant's city.

The *Office of Administrative Law Judge* holds independent, impartial hearings, similar to a civil trial, on cases involving the full range of HUD's administrative procedures. This office also hears and decides FHEO cases. Its ruling in a case is generally regarded as the final decision of the department.

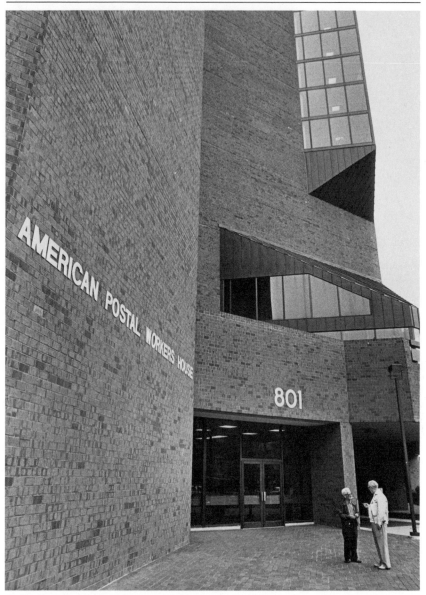

Two retired postal workers stop to chat outside their home, the American Postal Workers House in Philadelphia. The complex was built with the aid of HUD's Section 202 program, which has been effective at producing housing for senior citizens. Other HUD programs have had widely varying degrees of success.

SIX

HUD: Past, Present, and Future

Has the Department of Housing and Urban Development been successful in addressing the problems of urban America, particularly in the area of housing? A brief survey of the accomplishments—and failures—of the department's major programs, such as the FHA mortgage insurance program, public housing, and various community development grant programs, provides an overall account of how well HUD has performed its mission.

HUD's Record

Enacted in the mid-1930s, the FHA mortgage insurance program was incorporated into HUD when the department was created in 1965. By increasing the sheer volume of available mortgage credit, the FHA's mortgage insurance has made the American dream of homeownership possible for many more families. Further, the FHA's programs helped to reform the structure of residential financing, popularizing the low–down payment, long-term, uniform-payment home loan that is common today. In addition, the FHA stimulated the creation of the mass production home-building industry. Because home builders may be relatively certain that they will be able to find buyers for their products, they can plan and construct large, multiunit subdivisions, or housing developments. Finally, the FHA requires the houses it finances to meet strict standards for structural soundness, fire protection, sewage disposal, and other construction features; in this way, the FHA provides a kind of consumer protection for home buyers.

But despite these many significant benefits, the FHA is not without its critics. The vast majority of FHA-assisted homes have been built in the suburbs. By essentially financing the building of suburbia, the FHA has enticed large numbers of middle-income families from the cities, depriving urban areas of much-needed tax revenues. Indeed, the agency often has been criticized for providing extensive aid to the suburbs and their middle-class residents, while offering meager assistance to central cities populated by the poor.

Mark Gelfand, in his book *A Nation of Cities: The Federal Government and Urban America, 1933–1965*, points out that because the FHA was designed in the 1930s to be a profitable enterprise, it was mostly concerned with the safety of the mortgages it insured. Gelfand states: "Right from its inception, the agency 'red lined' vast areas of the inner cities, refusing to insure mortgages where the neighborhoods were blighted or susceptible to blight. This action practically guaranteed that these districts would deteriorate still further and drag the cities down with them." (*Redlining* refers to the practice of refusing to loan money in an area where the lender feels there is little chance of being repaid. Low-income areas populated by minorities are often redlined by banks.) In 1967, political commentator Martin F. Nolan summed up the feelings of many critics before and since: "This prejudice against the cities and in favor of suburbs is the most grievous federal sin for which HUD must atone."

The FHA's supporters respond that the agency was not created to help the poor but to revive home building and stimulate homeownership, and it has been extraordinarily successful in carrying out these two goals. The agency's defenders argue that the FHA should not be the scapegoat for the failures of federal programs, such as public housing, that were created to meet the housing needs of the poor. Like the FHA, these programs fall under the auspices of HUD.

Public housing in the United States is, in many ways, seriously flawed. The physical design of much public housing is itself problematic. Far too many public housing projects consist of depressingly sterile, monotonously massive, and architecturally bleak structures. Jarringly out of proportion to the rest of the urban environment, these cold, institutional-looking buildings seem more like high-rise barracks or prisons than homes. There is little wonder, then, that

Hopkinson House, built under the provisions of Section 220 and designed by noted architect I. M. Pei, rises in the Society Hill section of Philadelphia. Despite careful design, the scale of public housing projects often makes them look like out-of-place eyesores in a community.

81

many public housing occupants are sensitive to the word *project*; the very appearance of the buildings tends to stigmatize the people who live in them.

But the real problem with public housing has less to do with aesthetics than with attitudes. Americans maintain a grudging view of how much, what kind of, and perhaps most importantly, where housing should be built for the poor. Most middle-class people righteously deplore the "high-rise chicken coops" where "nobody should have to live." However, these same citizens vehemently object to plans for locating public housing developments in their suburbs, even if these projects are small and well designed. As a result, public housing is usually relegated to the urban slums, where it quickly becomes absorbed into the run-down environment. "All across America," President Nixon declared in 1973, "the federal government has become the biggest slumlord in history."

Middle-class taxpayers resent federal funds being spent to subsidize housing for the poor. Yet, although many do not realize it, middle-class homeowners themselves receive a subsidy from the government, because they are allowed to deduct interest paid on their mortgages from their federal income taxes. If, in 1973, Nixon had instituted a moratorium on this mortgage interest deduction, rather than on subsidized housing, he would have been faced with an enormous outcry from the suburban middle class. But because public housing's clientele is the urban poor, who tend to be unorganized and politically weak, the program is a ready target for budget cutters. Moreover, public housing is often perceived by many voters and politicians as "black housing"; much of the mainstream opposition to this politically unpopular program may stem from the racial tensions and hostilities that lie so near the core of American society.

As a consequence, public housing is chronically underfunded, and the needs of its residents are underserved. There is, in short, a serious lack of public housing. In New York City, for example, more than 200,000 families languished on the public housing waiting list in 1990; at the prevailing turnover rate, a family that joins the waiting list in 1990 can expect to move into its unit in about 40 years.

When opponents of public housing want to highlight the program's most spectacular failures, they point to St. Louis's notorious Pruett-Igoe project. Pruett-Igoe, a complex of 43 11-story buildings, was erected in the 1950s at a cost of $36 million. By 1970, however, 26 of the buildings were vacant and boarded up. The huge project had succumbed to crime and vandalism. Life there had become so miserable and unsafe that the city's poor refused to live there and preferred to remain in squalid tenements at higher rents. Pruett-Igoe had become a federally funded disaster area, in every way resembling the worst slums in the nation. In desperation, HUD secretary George Romney ordered the project torn down.

The sad state of Pruett-Igoe, although extreme, had many features in common with other public housing projects—a large number of poor, unstable, problem-riddled families concentrated in a cold, institutional structure, situated in the midst of an existing ghetto where jobs are scarce, demeaning, and low paying, without adequate funding for much-needed social services. This is simply a recipe for social disaster.

Public housing is not a popular program in Washington. To liberal politicians, it is a necessary evil; to conservative ones, it is an unqualified evil. But when it has worked as intended, the program has provided improved housing for thousands of poor families, who, with their limited resources, otherwise could not have afforded it. Moreover, public housing has been of great benefit to senior citizens. Many of its sensational failures, such as Pruett-Igoe, reflect deeply rooted social forces rather than flaws in the program. Certainly crime, vandalism, and antisocial behavior were not born in the housing projects but were already rampant in America's slums. Public housing may not have solved these problems, but it also did not cause them.

When the Reagan administration looked at public housing, it declined to continue the program at anywhere near its previous levels. Instead, the housing voucher system was instituted. Designed as the showpiece of the Reagan administration's housing program, it was supposed to be a market-oriented alternative to public housing. Under the system, the federal government provides poor families with direct cash subsidies so they can choose their own rental housing. From the first, critics predicted that in many cities there would not be enough affordable, vacant rental units to meet the demand, a fear that has been borne out in practice. Whereas the voucher program works well enough in a city such as Dallas, where there is a high vacancy rate, it works miserably in New York City, where the situation is quite the opposite. In New York, where the typical monthly stipend was around $250 at the end of the 1980s, 8 out of every 9 families on the city's public housing waiting list who were offered a voucher returned it. Rents on the private housing market are so high, and the vacancy rate is so low, that they are unable to use the federal stipend. For these families, it is back to the waiting list.

In the area of community development, HUD's urban rehabilitation and slum clearance goals often have conflicted with its housing mission, as in the case of the urban renewal program, which displaced slum residents and utilized their former neighborhoods for commercial development. Model Cities attempted to correct some of the worst flaws of urban renewal, but the Nixon administration

A poster on a bus touts the day-care provisions of the Model Cities program in Atlanta, Georgia. Despite its flaws, the HUD program was the first to try to deal with all aspects of inner-city problems in a coordinated manner.

ended the program in 1973, replacing it with the current system of community development block grants. Advocates of CDBGs point out that they have reduced much of the bureaucratic red tape that burdened the earlier system of categorical grants (which specified the purposes for which funds must be used), and that many more jurisdictions now receive federal assistance.

However, the elimination of categorical grants resulted in a shifting of program activities from central cities to suburbs, and within cities from lower-income to middle-income parts. A study conducted in 1976 by the Southern Regional Council, a nonprofit public interest group, concluded that in the use of CDBGs, "decisions are made by politicians who often have little regard for the concerns of low and moderate income citizens." Without specific guidelines on how these funds are to be applied, state and local officials are likely to shuttle CDBG money into more politically strategic and less socially urgent uses. For example, in the mid-1970s, a tennis court complex in an affluent section of Little Rock, Arkansas, was built with a $150,000 block grant. The city's program director felt this use of federal funds was politically justified.

Critics of CDBGs point out that local communities sometimes do not choose to address the urgent needs of their poorest residents with the funds. This British double-decker bus and its extravagantly costumed driver were funded with a CDBG in Richmond, Virginia.

"We must remember the needs of the people who vote," he insisted, "and poor people don't vote."

Because CDBGs can be used for any of a wide range of urban development purposes, housing is not always the top priority. Influential economic and political elites have been successful in promoting programs concerned with economic development and civic pride. When the bulk of CDBG money is taken up by these community development activities, housing, particularly for those at the lowest end of the income scale, all too frequently becomes an afterthought.

A legitimate question exists about whether local and state governments can commit themselves wholeheartedly to improving the living conditions of low- and moderate-income families—a goal that was mentioned no fewer than four times in the 1974 block grant law's statement of purpose. Indeed, HUD's first secretary, Robert C. Weaver, recalled that on many occasions city mayors thanked HUD for requiring them, through the earlier categorical programs, to do what they knew they should. Without pressure from the federal government and the strictures on how categorical grants could be spent, the mayors felt politically unable to devote the money to the neediest areas. In short, the CDBG system may grant too much leeway, allowing local politicians too many opportunities to ignore the needs of the poor.

But whatever their drawbacks, whatever their flaws, HUD's programs have served the housing needs of a great many Americans. Of course, there is no question that more can be done. And so, as with any federal department or agency, HUD's record is one of successes combined with failures, efficiency combined with waste, competence and concern combined with cynicism and fraud—never more so than during the presidency of Ronald Reagan and the stewardship of HUD secretary Samuel Pierce.

The Reagan-Pierce Years and the Future of HUD

During Reagan's eight-year administration, the Department of Housing and Urban Development seldom occupied the attention of the president—except with regard to how his budget cutters might trim HUD's funding and programs. One instance may be particularly instructive about Reagan's interest in the department. At a White House reception in June 1981, Reagan greeted Samuel Pierce by saying, "How are you, Mr. Mayor?" Pierce was understandably nonplussed. The president had failed to recognize his own HUD secretary—

the only black member of his cabinet—whom he had appointed not five months earlier! Reagan had evidently confused him with Marion Barry, the black mayor of Washington, D.C.

From the start of the Reagan-Pierce years (1981–89) HUD was beset by turmoil and political intrigue. "When Reagan came in," one high-ranking career civil servant recalled, "his people were paranoid. They were suspicious of the career people, and they thought that whatever it was, the private sector could do it better." The new administration installed political appointees to head HUD's regional and field offices. These appointees often replaced experienced career civil servants, who were posted to distant assignments on short notice, or otherwise pushed aside.

A previous HUD secretary, George Romney, once fought valiantly, but in the end unsuccessfully, to protect his department from the attacks of a conservative, hostile Nixon White House. Secretary Pierce, however, embraced the Reagan philosophy, dismantling programs, firing talented staffers, promoting less-qualified political favorites, and generally lowering employee morale and departmental efficiency. As secretary, Pierce was a disinterested, hands-off manager, whose reticence earned him the nickname Silent Sam from

HUD secretary Samuel Pierce (left) looks over construction plans in front of single-family homes purchased with FHA-insured mortgages. Pierce more often preferred a "hands-off" approach to management.

his subordinates. He would address meetings of senior HUD officials over a speakerphone from his office rather than appear in person. When he did speak publicly, he defended Reagan's budget cuts.

But however disquieting, this atmosphere of tension and unease within HUD was not the worst of it; in mid-1989, the department was rocked by charges of large-scale corruption. HUD was thrust into the public spotlight by the sensational case of Maryland real estate agent Marilyn Harrell. In the largest-ever single case involving theft of federal funds by an individual, Harrell, who had been hired by HUD to sell department-owned properties, siphoned off between $4.75 million and $5.67 million in proceeds from these sales. She claimed that she donated the bulk of the money to charity, for which the press dubbed her "Robin HUD," and kept, as she claimed, "less than 6 percent" for herself—a total that still would amount to no less than $285,000. Federal prosecutors acknowledged that some money did go to charity but charged that "her largest single charity was, by far, herself." In January 1990, Harrell pleaded guilty to stealing government property and failing to report income for taxes. She was sentenced on June 22, 1990, to between 27 and 46 months in prison.

The Robin HUD case was just the tip of the iceberg; it soon became clear that for eight years HUD's programs had been awash in corruption, fraud, embezzlement, and waste. A Texas real estate agent was indicted on 79 counts involving the theft of $2.5 million from the sales of 55 Dallas homes. A Washington, D.C., lawyer, who had acted as an agent for HUD, disappeared. Subsequently, more than $3 million was listed as missing. The FHA and the GNMA lost huge sums through mismanagement and fraud; according to HUD's inspector general, department officials as far back as 1985 ignored his warnings about questionable mortgage lenders. By September 1989, 700 criminal investigations already were under way into purported fraud, embezzlement, and bribery at HUD. At the same time, both the Justice Department and the Senate Ethics Committee began investigating claims that Senator Alfonse D'Amato of New York had used his influence to assist relatives, friends, business associates, and political contributors in obtaining HUD grants. The Justice Department tallied 140 HUD-related convictions in 1989. The total money lost was estimated at between $2.5 billion and $4 billion.

Especially fraught with influence peddling was the Section 8 Moderate Rehabilitation program, which is supposed to assist private developers in purchasing and refurbishing low- and moderate-income rental units. An internal HUD audit, released in April 1989, found that contracts worth millions of dollars had been steered to developers who had hired well-known, well-

Marilyn Harrell is escorted into the federal courthouse in Baltimore, Maryland, by her attorney Anthony Gallagher in December 1989. "Robin HUD" (as the press dubbed her) was found guilty of selling houses that belonged to HUD and giving the proceeds to the poor as well as pocketing some herself, after she realized no one at HUD kept track of such money.

connected Republicans as "consultants." The consultants lobbied high department officials, who, in turn, exerted pressure on subordinates to approve funding for the consultants' clients. A consultant's price tag for a few well-placed phone calls could be as much as $300,000; the developers paid this fee out of their HUD jackpots. In other words, HUD subsidized the lobbyists who had been pressuring the department for political favors. It was estimated that some $750 million in HUD funds were spent in this way. Among the high-profile Republicans who acted as highly paid consultants were former

Massachusetts senator Edward Brooke, former HUD secretary Carla Hills, and former interior secretary James Watt.

Testifying before the House Subcommittee on Government Operations in May 1989, Secretary Pierce insisted that he was a hands-off administrator and denied direct involvement in granting awards and favors. (On three occasions later in the year, Pierce refused to answer congressional questions, invoking the Fifth Amendment's protection against self-incrimination.) Indeed, as HUD's boss, Pierce preferred to delegate rather than wield power; from 1984 to 1987, much of the day-to-day running of the department was handled by his executive assistant, Deborah Gore Dean.

Former HUD colleagues testified that Dean, who also invoked the Fifth Amendment before Congress, used her position to parcel out millions to Republican party supporters. Silvio DeBartolomeis, a former acting assistant secretary of housing, told the subcommittee that Dean ordered him to approve Section 8 projects about which he had felt "uncomfortable" because "political influence" was involved in the decision-making process. "She said that she had the authority of the Secretary to order me to sign the documents," DeBartolomeis testified. "She indicated the Secretary was knowledgeable about what went on." Pierce denied this, suggesting that Dean alone was behind the political favoritism. But Representative Charles Schumer of New York maintained that in any event Pierce must be held responsible for the mess at HUD. "Either Pierce knew what was going on and should be condemned," Schumer argued, "or he didn't know what was going on and should be condemned."

By November 1989, the House Judiciary Committee's six-month probe into HUD was winding down. Faced with the possibility that Pierce may have been involved in wrongdoing but stymied by his (and 3 of his aides') refusal to testify, 19 Democratic committee members petitioned Attorney General Richard Thornburgh to request a special prosecutor. In February 1990, Thornburgh acceded. The following month, a special three-judge panel appointed a retired federal judge, Arlin M. Adams, as the special prosecutor responsible for investigating whether Pierce and other HUD officials during the Reagan administration had conspired to defraud the United States or commit any other crime. Initially, Adams was directed to probe for wrongdoing in only one of HUD's programs—the Moderate Rehabilitation program. By November 1990, both the attorney general of the United States and the House Government Operations Committee–Subcommittee on Housing had asked Adams to broaden the scope of his investigation to include irregularities in the UDAG program and the Secretary's Discretionary Fund.

Deborah Gore Dean listens to attorney Joseph DiGenova. The executive assistant to Pierce, Dean was accused of letting Republican party politics influence the disposition of HUD funds and awards.

The House subcommittee concluded in a report issued on November 1, 1990, that "at best Pierce misled the Congressional committees and at worst may have committed perjury" in his testimony in May 1989. A November 2, 1990, article in *New York Newsday* noted that the subcommittee report "bolstered contentions that Pierce improperly assisted his former law firm in securing HUD funding for its clients' development projects." The report charged that during Pierce's tenure as HUD secretary, the department's projects were pursued with "blatant favoritism, political influence and abuse." It described the Moderate Rehabilitation program as "a cash cow which was milked by former HUD officials and the politically well-connected." However, the subcommittee stopped short of asserting that Pierce had behaved illegally.

Meanwhile, HUD secretary Jack Kemp proposed a package of 50 reforms aimed at "clearing the decks" at the scandal-plagued department he inherited when President Bush appointed him in February 1989. Some of these reforms had to be passed by Congress; others required administrative action. Among the changes at HUD were the following:

- Publishing of all funding decisions in the *Federal Register*. (The *Federal Register* is the U.S. government's official compilation of notices issued by federal agencies, presidential proclamations, and executive orders. Continually updated, it is available at public libraries and from the government.)
- Requiring registration of HUD consultants and disclosing their fees.
- Appointment of a chief financial officer to oversee HUD.
- Redirecting CDBGs to low- and moderate-income areas.
- Overhauling the FHA through stricter auditing and tougher standards for outside agents.

"I will not allow HUD's mission to be paralyzed," Kemp declared, describing his reform package as a "redirection" away from high-paid consultants and "back to the poor."

In January 1990, Kemp suspended five top housing managers in Passaic, New Jersey, for "grossly excessive" salaries and other abuses. A HUD report said that in 1988 the executive director in Passaic was paid $245,956, more than double the secretary's salary. HUD investigators cited a total of $1.68 million in ineligible and unsupported costs; the local officials responded that HUD had approved their compensation levels. These suspensions—the first during Kemp's tenure—were intended to warn others that the practices of the Reagan-Pierce era would not be allowed to continue.

In fiscal year 1991, the Bush administration launched the cornerstone of its housing policy (in fact, the only major housing initiative of its first two years), a new program called Homeownership and Opportunity for People Everywhere (HOPE). Its mission, as described in the *Budget of the United States Government, Fiscal Year 1991*, is "to help low income families become homeowners with a stake in their communities." This program provides federal funds, called HOPE grants, that enable public housing residents to manage their own buildings and eventually purchase the units in which they live. In the words of Secretary Kemp, "We're trying to empower the people themselves." States, localities, or nonprofit organizations must provide $1 for every $2 of federal funds dispensed. The money may be used to pay for rehabilitation, acquisition, technical assistance, security, and mortgage assistance, but not for the construction of new units.

Many Democrats in Congress, recalling the hostility of previous Republican presidents toward public housing, were skeptical of the Bush administration's new program. Some liberal legislators wondered if it was merely a means to cut this unpopular, though necessary, program even further. Representative Schumer, for example, feared that it would prove to be "more hype than hope."

Specifically, congressional critics objected that HOPE provides no money for new construction and cuts support for modernization of public housing. Senator Alan Cranston of California, noting the current shortage of low-cost rental units, argued, "We need new housing, we've got too many people and not enough homes." The Democrats did feel that HOPE was worth a try but cautioned that it simply did not do enough to solve the nation's housing problems. As Representative Henry Gonzales of Texas, the chairperson of the House Banking and Urban Affairs Committee, told Secretary Kemp, "Your proposals, as laudable as they are, may be unrealistic and unworkable as the foundation of the nation's housing policy."

As the 1990s began, HUD's image with Congress and the voters had been seriously damaged. Clearly, the department's ability to serve the nation's housing needs would be hampered by the mounting revelations of eight years' worth of mismanagement and corruption. Senator Bob Graham of Florida cautioned that HUD would have to "meet a new level of credibility" before Congress would back major new housing programs. "The first job," Representative Schumer agreed, "is to clean up the mess." The nation's ill housed and homeless would have to wait.

Indeed, for fiscal year 1991, Congress allocated just more than $23 billion for HUD's budget, virtually the same amount that the department received in fiscal 1990. Normally, Congress will increase a department's budget each year. When that does not happen, it is a sure sign that the department in question is facing the scrutiny of the legislative branch, and that its activities—even its very mission—are in jeopardy.

Many HUD programs, including the scandal-ridden Moderate Rehabilitation program, were cut. With federal investigators keeping a close watch on every level of HUD activity, local HUD officials, fearing charges of influence peddling, became more wary and placed many projects on hold.

Many political observers noted that the decade of the 1980s was marked by a significant rise in the number of ill-housed and homeless people living in the

HUD secretary Jack Kemp speaks to young urbanites during a visit to a Federal Enterprise Zone. Faced with the HUD scandals of the 1980s, Kemp immediately set to work reforming the troubled department. His success or failure will affect not only the lives of these children but also the lives of millions of Americans, for the growing problems of U.S. cities are the growing problems of the nation.

United States. "While homelessness grew to be an epidemic in America," Schumer lamented, "the federal agency in charge became a swamp of fraud and favoritism." And so, more than 40 years later, the aim of the Housing Act of 1949—"a decent home and a suitable living environment for every American family"—seemed more distant than ever. Worse, this mission had been compromised by the agency that, in 1965, was created to carry it out, the Department of Housing and Urban Development.

Department of Housing and Urban Development

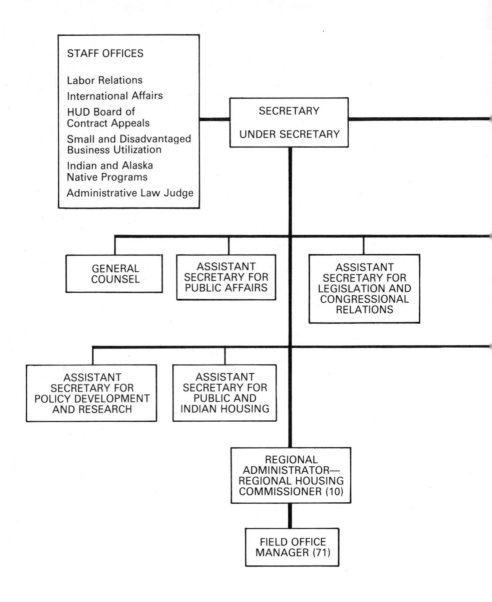

STAFF OFFICES

Labor Relations

International Affairs

HUD Board of
Contract Appeals

Small and Disadvantaged
Business Utilization

Indian and Alaska
Native Programs

Administrative Law Judge

SECRETARY

UNDER SECRETARY

GENERAL
COUNSEL

ASSISTANT
SECRETARY FOR
PUBLIC AFFAIRS

ASSISTANT
SECRETARY FOR
LEGISLATION AND
CONGRESSIONAL
RELATIONS

ASSISTANT
SECRETARY FOR
POLICY DEVELOPMENT
AND RESEARCH

ASSISTANT
SECRETARY FOR
PUBLIC AND
INDIAN HOUSING

REGIONAL
ADMINISTRATOR—
REGIONAL HOUSING
COMMISSIONER (10)

FIELD OFFICE
MANAGER (71)

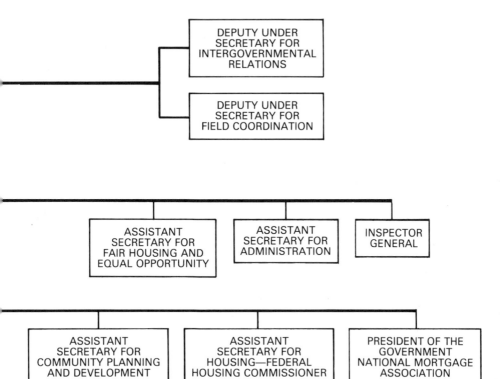

DEPUTY UNDER
SECRETARY FOR
INTERGOVERNMENTAL
RELATIONS

DEPUTY UNDER
SECRETARY FOR
FIELD COORDINATION

ASSISTANT
SECRETARY FOR
FAIR HOUSING AND
EQUAL OPPORTUNITY

ASSISTANT
SECRETARY FOR
ADMINISTRATION

INSPECTOR
GENERAL

ASSISTANT
SECRETARY FOR
COMMUNITY PLANNING
AND DEVELOPMENT

ASSISTANT
SECRETARY FOR
HOUSING—FEDERAL
HOUSING COMMISSIONER

PRESIDENT OF THE
GOVERNMENT
NATIONAL MORTGAGE
ASSOCIATION

GLOSSARY

Block grants   Federal funds distributed by HUD that may be used for unspecified purposes within a general area, such as education, transportation, or urban improvement.

Categorical grants   Federal funds distributed by HUD that must be used only for specific purposes.

Collateral   The property a borrower promises to a lender if the loan is not repaid. (See *Foreclosure*)

Default   Failure to repay a loan.

Eminent domain   The right of government to appropriate private property for public use, after financially compensating the property's owner.

Entitlement grants   Federal funds distributed annually by HUD to cities with populations of more than 50,000 and urban counties with populations of more than 200,000. Such areas are entitled to the funds by law.

Federal Housing Administration (FHA)   The federal agency, created in 1934, that administers the government's mortgage insurance programs.

Federal National Mortgage Association (FNMA)   An institution that buys and sells mortgages that have been made by private lenders. Popularly known as Fannie Mae, it was created as an independent federal agency in 1938 but in 1968 became a private corporation operating under the guidance of the HUD secretary.

Federal Register   The U.S. government's official compilation of notices issued by federal agencies, presidential proclamations, and executive orders. Continually updated, it is available at public libraries and from the government.

Foreclosure   The seizure of collateral when a borrower defaults on a loan. (See *Collateral*)

Government National Mortgage Association (GNMA)   An agency within HUD that attracts funds into the mortgage market by guaranteeing the securities that private lenders issue and sell. It is popularly known as Ginnie Mae.

Housing and Home Finance Agency (HHFA) Established in 1947, it was the first permanent federal agency to coordinate all of the government's nonfarm housing programs. The agency was the direct precursor of HUD.

Housing starts New houses under construction at a given time.

Laissez-faire The theory that the government should not intervene in running the economy.

Model Cities Enacted in 1966, an ambitious program designed to correct the worst flaws of urban renewal and to demonstrate the benefits of a coordinated federal approach to the problems of cities. The program was ended by President Nixon's 1973 housing moratorium.

Moratorium A freeze or suspension of action. In 1973, President Nixon declared a moratorium on urban renewal, Model Cities, and all subsidized housing programs.

Nonentitlement grants Federal funds allocated by HUD to individual states, which in turn award grants to smaller communities based on a combination of demographic and economic factors.

Public housing Federally subsidized rental housing for low-income families.

Redlining The practice of refusing to loan money in an area where the lender feels there is little chance of being repaid. Low-income areas populated by minorities are often redlined by banks.

Staff-year The working time and paid leave of one employee for one year.

Urban blight The economic and physical deterioration of areas within a city.

Urban renewal A large-scale federal program of slum clearance and urban redevelopment inaugurated by the Housing Act of 1949. President Nixon ended the controversial program in 1973.

SELECTED REFERENCES

Bernotas, Bob. *The Federal Government: How It Works.* New York: Chelsea House, 1990.

Cleaveland, Frederic N., and associates. *Congress and Urban Problems.* Washington, DC: The Brookings Institution, 1969.

Fried, Joseph P. *Housing Crisis U.S.A.* Baltimore: Penguin Books, 1972.

Gans, Herbert J. "The Failure of Urban Renewal: A Critique and Some Proposals." *Commentary* 39, no. 4 (April 1965): pp. 29–37.

Gelfand, Mark I. *A Nation of Cities: The Federal Government and Urban America, 1933–1965.* New York: Oxford University Press, 1975.

Hays, R. Allen. *The Federal Government and Urban Housing: Ideology and Change in Public Policy.* Albany: State University of New York Press, 1985.

Lord, Tom Forrester. *Decent Housing: A Promise to Keep.* Cambridge, MA: Schenkman Publishing, 1977.

Mason, Joseph B. *History of Housing in the U.S., 1930–1980.* Houston: Gulf Publishing, 1982.

McFarland, M. Carter. *Federal Government and Urban Problems—HUD: Successes, Failures, and the Fate of Our Cities.* Boulder, CO: Westview Press, 1978.

U.S. Department of Housing and Urban Development, Office of Administration. *Profile of HUD.* Washington, DC: U.S. Department of Housing and Urban Development, 1989.

U.S. Department of Housing and Urban Development. *Programs of HUD, 1988–1989.* Washington, DC: U.S. Department of Housing and Urban Development, 1989.

Winerip, Michael. "In New York, HUD's Vouchers Pay for Already Cheap Housing." *The New York Times,* December 31, 1989.

INDEX

Adams, Arlin M., 90
American City, 30
American Federation of Labor
and Congress of Industrial
Organizations (AFL-CIO), 49

Balloon payments, 26
Barry, Marion, 87
Black Panthers, 41
Brooke, Edward, 90
*Budget of the United States
Government, Fiscal Year
1991,* 92
Bush, George, 92, 93
Buttenheim, Harold S., 30

Carter, Jimmy, 52
Civil Rights Act of 1964, 42
Civil Rights Act of 1968, 62, 74
Civil War, U.S., 40
Clark, Joseph, 31
Commerce, Department of, 16,
18, 39
Commission on Metropolitan
Problems and Urban Devel-
opment, 31
Community development block
grants (CDBGs), 51, 52, 71–
72, 83, 86
Community Facilities Adminis-
tration, 31
Competitive Service, 58
Congress, U.S., 23–25, 31, 41,
50, 62, 93
Congressional Budget Office
(CBO), 62
Cranston, Alan, 93

D'Amato, Alfonse, 88
Dean, Deborah Gore, 90
DeBartolomeis, Silvio, 90
Defense, Department of, 20

Democratic party, 36, 40, 52,
55, 93
"Department of Urbiculture,"
30–31, 39

Education, Department of, 17
Eisenhower, Dwight David,
29
Energy, Department of, 17
Entitlement grants, 71
Ehrlichman, John, 48
Excepted Service, 57

Fair Housing Amendments Act
of 1988, 74
Fannie Mae. *See* Federal Na-
tional Mortgage Association
Farmers Home Administration
(FmHA), 65
Fascell, Dante, 31–32
Federal Enterprise Zone pro-
gram, 73
Federal Housing Administra-
tion (FHA), 21, 26, 28, 64,
67, 68, 80
Federal National Mortgage
Association (FNMA), 31, 58,
69
Federal Register, 92
Ford, Gerald, 50, 51
Foreclosure, 24

Gelfand, Mark, 80
General Accounting Office
(GAO), 61
General Services Administra-
tion (GSA), 62, 75
Ginnie Mae. *See* Government
National Mortgage Associa-
tion
Goldwater, Barry, 40
Gonzales, Henry, 93

Bob Bernotas is a freelance writer living in Brooklyn, NY. He holds a Ph.D. in political theory from the Johns Hopkins University and has taught philosophy and political science at Morgan State and Towson State Universities. His published works include a study guide for a textbook on American government, numerous articles on jazz and sports, and *The Federal Government: How It Works,* a volume in Chelsea House's KNOW YOUR GOVERNMENT series.

Arthur M. Schlesinger, jr., served in the White House as special assistant to Presidents Kennedy and Johnson. He is the author of numerous acclaimed works in American history and has twice been awarded the Pulitzer Prize. He taught history at Harvard College for many years and is currently Albert Schweitzer Professor of the Humanities at the City College of New York.

GAYLORD M2